Company's Coming®

Slow Cooker Dinners

Jean Paré

companyscoming.com
visit our website

Front Cover

1. Pesto Chicken Pasta, page 44
2. Chunky Vegetable Chili, page 116
3. Rice And Bean Tacos, page 112

Props Courtesy Of:
Hamilton Beach® Canada
The Bay

Back Cover

1. Sweet And Sour Pork, page 75
2. Snappy Pineapple Chicken, page 42
3. Chinese Mushroom Soup, page 77

Props Courtesy Of:
Pier 1 Imports
Scona Clayworks

We gratefully acknowledge the following suppliers for their generous support of our Test Kitchen and Photo Studio:

Broil King Barbecues — *Lagostina®*
Corelle® — *Proctor Silex® Canada*
Hamilton Beach® Canada — *Tupperware®*

Slow Cooker Dinners

First Printing February 2005

Library and Archives Canada Cataloguing in Publication

Paré, Jean
Slow cooker dinners / Jean Paré.

Includes index.
ISBN 1-896891-69-1

1. Electric cookery, Slow. I. Title.

TX827.P368 2005   641.5'884   C2004-905945-9

Published by
Company's Coming Publishing Limited
2311 – 96 Street
Edmonton, Alberta, Canada T6N 1G3
Tel: 780-450-6223 Fax: 780-450-1857
www.companyscoming.com

Printed in Canada

Table of Contents

The Company's Coming Story

Jean Paré grew up understanding that the combination of family, friends and home cooking is the essence of a good life. From her mother she learned to appreciate good cooking, while her father praised even her earliest attempts. When she left home she took with her many acquired family recipes, a love of cooking and an intriguing desire to read recipe books like novels!

"never share a recipe you wouldn't use yourself"

In 1963, when her four children had all reached school age, Jean volunteered to cater the 50th anniversary of the Vermilion School of Agriculture, now Lakeland College. Working out of her home, Jean prepared a dinner for over 1000 people which launched a flourishing catering operation that continued for over eighteen years. During that time she was provided with countless opportunities to test new ideas with immediate feedback—resulting in empty plates and contented customers! Whether preparing cocktail sandwiches for a house party or serving a hot meal for 1500 people, Jean Paré earned a reputation for good food, courteous service and reasonable prices.

"Why don't you write a cookbook?" Time and again, as requests for her recipes mounted, Jean was asked that question. Jean's response was to team up with her son, Grant Lovig, in the fall of 1980 to form Company's Coming Publishing Limited. April 14, 1981 marked the debut of "150 DELICIOUS SQUARES," the first Company's Coming cookbook in what soon would become Canada's most popular cookbook series.

Jean Paré's operation has grown steadily from the early days of working out of a spare bedroom in her home. Full-time staff includes marketing personnel located in major cities across Canada. Home Office is based in Edmonton, Alberta in a modern building constructed specially for the company.

Today the company distributes throughout Canada and the United States in addition to numerous overseas markets, all under the guidance of Jean's daughter, Gail Lovig. Best-sellers many times over in English, Company's Coming cookbooks have also been published in French and Spanish. Familiar and trusted in home kitchens around the world, Company's Coming cookbooks are offered in a variety of formats, including the original softcover series.

Jean Paré's approach to cooking has always called for quick and easy recipes using everyday ingredients. Even when travelling, she is constantly on the lookout for new ideas to share with her readers. At home, she can usually be found researching and writing recipes, or working in the company's test kitchen. Jean continues to gain new supporters by adhering to what she calls "the golden rule of cooking:" never share a recipe you wouldn't use yourself. It's an approach that works—*millions of times over!*

Foreword

The tremendous popularity of our *Slow Cooker Recipes* book continues to astound us. In answer to the many reader requests we've had for a sequel, *Slow Cooker Dinners* was born.

Find more than 115 all-new, kitchen-tested, Guaranteed Great™ recipes inside. That's more than 115 ways to save time when it matters most—at the end of a hectic day.

Recipe preparation can easily be done the evening before, or first thing in the morning. Then just turn on the slow cooker and go about your day. Arrive home to the tantalizing aroma of a delicious hot meal. What could be better than that?

Most recipes in *Slow Cooker Dinners* can be cooked on either a High or Low setting, so you can choose to cook for 4 to 5 hours or for 8 to 10. The Low setting is great when time allows, particularly for tenderizing meat. The High setting is best when you're running errands or simply relaxing while the slow cooker takes care of dinner for you.

There are many foods you probably didn't think you could prepare in a slow cooker. Would you believe it's an ideal way to cook steak and ribs? Try a new version of some old favourites such as a stew, soup, casserole or chili. Check out our hearty meals using beef, pork, lamb, chicken and turkey, as well as recipes with legumes and a section for meatless meals. There's also a small quantity section that's ideal when cooking for one or two.

Did you know that meat shrinks less in a slow cooker? That makes it perfect for those economical cuts, saving you both money and time! Did you know slow cookers heat from the sides and not the bottom? That's perfect for more even cooking. For General Slow Cooking Tips, see page 9.

Pull out your slow cooker and enjoy a flavourful, tender meal tonight with the help of *Slow Cooker Dinners*! It's like having your own personal cook welcome you home with dinner ready for the table. Enjoy the break!

Jean Paré

Nutrition Information Guidelines

Each recipe is analyzed using the most current version of the Canadian Nutrient File from Health Canada, which is based on the United States Department of Agriculture (USDA) Nutrient Database.

- If more than one ingredient is listed (such as "hard margarine or butter"), or if a range is given (1 – 2 tsp., 5 – 10 mL), only the first ingredient or first amount is analyzed.
- For meat, poultry and fish, the serving size per person is based on the recommended 4 oz. (113 g) uncooked weight (without bone), which is 2 – 3 oz. (57 – 85 g) cooked weight (without bone)— approximately the size of a deck of playing cards.
- Milk used is 1% M.F. (milk fat), unless otherwise stated.
- Cooking oil used is canola oil, unless otherwise stated.
- Ingredients indicating "sprinkle," "optional," or "for garnish" are not included in the nutrition information.

Margaret Ng, B.Sc. (Hon.), M.A.
Registered Dietitian

Get To Know Your Slow Cooker

Your slow cooker should have instructions explaining how to use it, how cooking times can vary between different brands, and how high altitude and fluctuations in power can affect your slow cooker. Read instructions carefully. As soon as you cook a few meals, you'll know your slow cooker well enough to compensate for any snags. Slow cookers use only a little electricity so they're a cost-effective way to cook.

The heating coils in slow cookers are around the side, not on the bottom, so foods are less likely to burn and moisture doesn't evaporate as rapidly. As a rule most slow cookers have only two settings—High and Low. Some may also have a Keep Warm setting. Your instruction booklet will confirm the use of each setting.

Food Safety Tips

To ensure safe cooking, we've compiled these helpful tips.

- Thaw frozen food before cooking for accurate cooking times.
- Don't lift lid while food is cooking as heat and moisture are released and this adds extra time to cooking. Add 20 to 30 minutes to your time whenever you have to lift the lid.
- When assembling ingredients in slow cooker liner the night before, cool liquids that have been heated during preparation to prevent bacteria from growing. Chill fully cooked meat for the same reason before assembling in slow cooker liner. Keep raw meat in separate container. Chill, then assemble with other ingredients just before cooking.
- Don't let ingredients warm to room temperature before cooking to prevent bacterial growth. Keep ingredients in separate containers in refrigerator until ready to assemble.
- Don't partially cook meat or poultry and then chill in refrigerator as this causes bacteria to grow. Our make-ahead instructions keep food safety in mind, so follow them exactly.
- Test doneness of poultry or large pieces of meat with meat thermometer to ensure proper temperature has been reached.
- Don't reheat food in slow cooker because the temperature doesn't get hot enough quickly enough to get food out of the bacteria danger zone.
- Chill foods soon after serving to prevent bacterial growth. Don't let cooked foods stand at room temperature for more than 2 hours.

General Slow Cooking Tips

Each recipe in this book offers directions for preparing a specific dish. However, here are some general tips to keep in mind when using a slow cooker:

- Fill slow cooker at least half full with food so the heat will be distributed more evenly.
- Layer food so root vegetables (such as carrots, turnips, potatoes) are on bottom, followed by meat, seasoning, then non-root vegetables (such as peas, corn, mushrooms). This keeps food moist and ensures more even cooking.
- With a lower cooking temperature, liquids don't evaporate as much so vegetables and meat are less likely to dry out. You may have to add more herbs or spices because the flavour will be diluted, or you may reduce amount of liquid used. When following the recipes in this book, these adjustments have been made for cooking on Low.
- Use dried herbs or spices during longer cooking times and add fresh herbs or spices when cooking is almost complete.
- Dairy products should be added close to end of cooking time as they can separate and look curdled when cooked for too long.
- If you miss the scheduled end of your cooking time on Low, an extra hour or so won't hurt. Be careful of extra time when cooking on High or when cooking pasta, as pasta has a tendency to become overcooked. We prefer to cook pasta separately so it maintains its shape and flavour.
- To prevent white meat from drying out, keep skin on to lock in moisture then remove before serving. Darker meat, such as thighs and legs, cooks slower than white meat so it may help to keep near bottom of slow cooker.
- As an economical alternative for those recipes calling for boneless, skinless chicken, substitute same number of bone-in, skinless chicken pieces. After slow cooking, the meat may be falling off the bones so be careful when serving, as small bones may not be visible in the sauce.
- Meat should be well trimmed of fat before adding to slow cooker to reduce fat.
- Pre-browning meat is recommended. It adds flavour and colour to the dish. But if time won't allow, meat (except ground meat) can be added without pre-browning.
- Make slow cooker meals delectable by sprinkling chopped fresh herbs, tomato, green onion, grated cheese or crumbs on top before serving.

Garden Bounty Beef

A great ground beef dish! Slightly sweet, tomatoey sauce with bountiful chunks of zucchini, carrot and red pepper. Wonderful served over rice, noodles or an open-face bun.

Sliced zucchini (with peel)	**5 cups**	**1.25 L**
Can of condensed tomato soup	**10 oz.**	**284 mL**
Chopped onion	**1 cup**	**250 mL**
Sliced carrot	**1 cup**	**250 mL**
Frozen kernel corn	**1 cup**	**250 mL**
Medium tomatoes, diced	**3**	**3**
Chili powder	**2 tsp.**	**10 mL**
Granulated sugar	**1 tsp.**	**5 mL**
Dried whole oregano	**1/4 tsp.**	**1 mL**
Salt	**1/2 tsp.**	**2 mL**
Pepper	**1/4 tsp.**	**1 mL**
Cooking oil	**1 tsp.**	**5 mL**
Lean ground beef	**1 lb.**	**454 g**
Frozen peas	**1 cup**	**250 mL**
Diced red pepper	**1/4 cup**	**60 mL**

Combine first 11 ingredients in 3 1/2 to 4 quart (3.5 to 4 L) slow cooker.

Heat cooking oil in large frying pan on medium. Add ground beef. Scramble-fry for 5 to 10 minutes until no longer pink. Drain. Add to zucchini mixture. Stir well. Cover. Cook on Low for 8 to 10 hours or on High for 4 to 5 hours.

Add peas and red pepper. Stir well. Cover. Cook on High for 10 to 15 minutes until peas are heated through and red pepper is tender-crisp. Serves 4.

1 serving: *390 Calories; 13.1 g Total Fat (5.2 g Mono, 1.8 g Poly, 4.2 g Sat); 59 mg Cholesterol; 44 g Carbohydrate; 10 g Fibre; 29 g Protein; 963 mg Sodium*

Pictured on page 18.

Make Ahead: The night before, assemble first 11 ingredients, as directed, in slow cooker liner. Cover. Chill overnight. Scramble-fry ground beef until no longer pink. Drain. Chill overnight in covered bowl. Assemble and cook as directed.

Swiss Steak

An old favourite, sure to satisfy. Serve this tender beef and savoury sauce with mashed potatoes and crusty bread—a hearty meal!

Sliced onion	**2 cups**	**500 mL**
Sliced carrot	**1 cup**	**250 mL**
Sliced celery	**1 cup**	**250 mL**
All-purpose flour	**2 tbsp.**	**30 mL**
Salt	**1/4 tsp.**	**1 mL**
Pepper	**1/4 tsp.**	**1 mL**
Boneless round steak, trimmed of fat and cut into 8 pieces	**2 lbs.**	**900 g**
Cooking oil	**1 tbsp.**	**15 mL**
Prepared beef broth	**1/2 cup**	**125 mL**
All-purpose flour	**2 tbsp.**	**30 mL**
Can of Roma (plum) tomatoes (with juice), tomatoes cut in half	**14 oz.**	**398 mL**
Dried thyme	**1/2 tsp.**	**2 mL**

Layer first 3 ingredients, in order given, in 3 1/2 to 4 quart (3 to 4 L) slow cooker.

Combine next 3 ingredients in large resealable freezer bag. Add 1/2 of beef. Seal bag. Toss until coated. Repeat with remaining beef. Heat cooking oil in large frying pan on medium-high. Add beef in 2 batches. Cook for 2 to 3 minutes per batch, stirring occasionally, until browned. Layer on top of celery.

Stir broth into second amount of flour in medium bowl until smooth. Add tomatoes and thyme. Stir well. Pour over beef. Do not stir. Cover. Cook on Low for 8 to 10 hours or on High for 4 to 5 hours. Serves 8.

1 serving: *198 Calories; 6.3 g Total Fat (2.9 g Mono, 0.8 g Poly, 1.6 g Sat); 52 mg Cholesterol; 12 g Carbohydrate; 2 g Fibre; 23 g Protein; 271 mg Sodium*

Make Ahead: The night before, layer first 3 ingredients, in order given, in slow cooker liner. Cover. Chill overnight. Trim and cut up uncooked beef. Chill overnight in covered bowl. Assemble and cook as directed.

Meatballs And Snow Peas

A great meal that's quick and easy to prepare. Adding snow peas just before serving keeps them tender-crisp. Serve with rice.

MINI-MEATBALLS		
Finely chopped onion	1/2 cup	125 mL
Fine dry bread crumbs	1/4 cup	60 mL
Large egg	1	1
Parsley flakes	1 tsp.	5 mL
Salt	1/2 tsp.	2 mL
Pepper	1/4 tsp.	1 mL
Lean ground beef	1 lb.	454 g
Can of pineapple tidbits (with juice)	14 oz.	398 mL
Thinly sliced carrot	1/2 cup	125 mL
Brown sugar, packed	1/2 cup	125 mL
White vinegar	1/3 cup	75 mL
Ketchup	1/4 cup	60 mL
Soy sauce	3 tbsp.	50 mL
Water	3 tbsp.	50 mL
Finely grated, peeled gingerroot (or 1/2 tsp., 2 mL, ground ginger)	2 tsp.	10 mL
Garlic clove, minced (or 1/4 tsp., 1 mL, powder)	1	1
Water	1 tbsp.	15 mL
Cornstarch	2 tsp.	10 mL
Snow peas, trimmed	1 cup	250 mL
Thinly sliced green onion	1 tbsp.	15 mL

Mini-Meatballs: Combine first 6 ingredients in medium bowl.

Add ground beef. Mix well. Roll mixture into 1 inch (2.5 cm) balls, using 1 tbsp. (15 mL) for each. Makes about 40 meatballs. Arrange evenly spaced apart on greased baking sheet with sides. Broil 6 inches (15 cm) from heat in oven for about 15 minutes, turning meatballs at halftime, until no longer pink inside.

(continued on next page)

Combine next 9 ingredients in 3 1/2 to 4 quart (3.5 to 4 L) slow cooker. Add meatballs. Stir gently. Cover. Cook on Low for 8 to 10 hours or on High for 4 to 5 hours.

Stir water into cornstarch in small cup until smooth. Add to meatball mixture. Stir gently. Cover. Cook on High for 10 to 15 minutes until sauce is slightly thickened.

Add snow peas and green onion. Stir. Cover. Cook for about 5 minutes until snow peas are just tender-crisp. Serves 4.

1 serving: *534 Calories; 19.1 g Total Fat (8.1 g Mono, 1.1 g Poly, 7.4 g Sat); 118 mg Cholesterol; 65 g Carbohydrate; 3 g Fibre; 27 g Protein; 1451 mg Sodium*

Pictured on page 18.

Make Ahead: The night before, prepare and cook meatballs until no longer pink inside. Drain. Chill overnight in covered bowl. Prepare pineapple mixture. Chill overnight in separate covered bowl. Assemble and cook as directed.

tip *When recipe doesn't call for a whole can of tomato paste, freeze unopened can for 30 minutes. Open both ends and push contents through, slicing off only what you need. Freeze remaining contents in resealable freezer bag.*

Ginger Beef Stew

A taste of the Far East. Thick ginger sauce coats tender beef, water chestnuts and snow peas. Great served over rice noodles.

Medium onions, cut into wedges	**2**	**2**
Medium carrot, sliced diagonally	**1**	**1**
Can of sliced water chestnuts, drained	**8 oz.**	**227 mL**
Roasted red peppers, drained and blotted dry, cut into strips	**1 cup**	**250 mL**
Cooking oil	**1 tbsp.**	**15 mL**
Inside round steak, trimmed of fat and cut into 1/2 inch (12 mm) pieces	**1 1/2 lbs.**	**680 g**
Finely grated, peeled gingerroot (or 1 1/2 tsp., 7 mL, ground ginger)	**2 tbsp.**	**30 mL**
Garlic cloves, minced (or 1/2 tsp., 2 mL, powder)	**2**	**2**
Water	**2/3 cup**	**150 mL**
Dry sherry (or beef broth)	**1/4 cup**	**60 mL**
Brown sugar, packed	**1 tbsp.**	**15 mL**
Soy sauce	**3 tbsp.**	**50 mL**
Cornstarch	**1 tbsp.**	**15 mL**
Snow peas, trimmed	**1 cup**	**250 mL**

Layer first 4 ingredients, in order given, in 3 1/2 to 4 quart (3.5 to 4 L) slow cooker.

Heat cooking oil in large frying pan on medium. Add beef. Cook for 8 to 10 minutes, stirring occasionally, until browned.

Add ginger and garlic. Heat and stir for about 1 minute until fragrant.

Add water, sherry and brown sugar. Stir. Bring to a boil. Pour over vegetables. Do not stir. Cover. Cook on Low for 8 to 9 hours or on High for 4 to 4 1/2 hours.

Stir soy sauce into cornstarch in small cup until smooth. Add to beef mixture. Stir. Add snow peas. Stir well. Cover. Cook on High for about 10 minutes until snow peas are tender-crisp and sauce is thickened. Serves 6.

(continued on next page)

1 serving: *266 Calories; 8.4 g Total Fat (3.7 g Mono, 1 g Poly, 2.2 g Sat); 53 mg Cholesterol; 17 g Carbohydrate; 2 g Fibre; 28 g Protein; 603 mg Sodium*

Pictured on page 36.

Make Ahead: The night before, prepare vegetables (except snow peas). Layer, in order given, in slow cooker liner. Cover. Chill overnight. Trim and cut up beef. Chill overnight in covered bowl. Assemble and cook as directed.

Beef With Onion Sauce

Moist, tender beef cooked to perfection in a flavourful jus. Serve with mashed potatoes, rice or noodles.

Boneless cross-rib roast	**3 – 4 lbs.**	**1.4 – 1.8 kg**
Cooking oil	**2 tsp.**	**10 mL**
Sliced onion	**1 cup**	**250 mL**
Prepared beef broth	**1/2 cup**	**125 mL**
Dijon mustard	**1 tbsp.**	**15 mL**
Worcestershire sauce	**1 tbsp.**	**15 mL**
Bay leaves	**2**	**2**
Water	**3 tbsp.**	**50 mL**
All-purpose flour	**2 tbsp.**	**30 mL**

Place roast in 4 to 5 quart (4 to 5 L) slow cooker.

Heat cooking oil in medium frying pan on medium. Add onion. Cook for 5 to 10 minutes, stirring often, until softened.

Add next 4 ingredients. Stir well. Pour over roast. Cover. Cook on Low for 8 to 10 hours or on High for 4 to 5 hours. Remove roast to large serving platter. Cover to keep warm. Remove and discard bay leaves.

Stir water into flour in small cup until smooth. Add to liquid in slow cooker. Stir well. Cover. Cook on High for about 10 minutes until slightly thickened. Carefully process with hand blender or in blender until smooth. Makes about 3 cups (750 mL) sauce. Cut roast into thin slices. Serve with sauce. Makes 12 servings (2 to 3 oz., 57 to 85 g each, cooked weight).

1 serving: *277 Calories; 19.2 g Total Fat (8.3 g Mono, 1 g Poly, 7.5 g Sat); 63 mg Cholesterol; 2 g Carbohydrate; trace Fibre; 22 g Protein; 129 mg Sodium*

Corned Beef Dinner

Tender corned beef and winter vegetables make a comforting meal. Strain and save the broth to use in your favourite soup recipe.

Baby carrots	**1 lb.**	**454 g**
Red baby potatoes, larger ones cut in half	**1 lb.**	**454 g**
Yellow medium turnip, cut into 1 inch (2.5 cm) cubes	**1**	**1**
Chopped onion	**2 cups**	**500 mL**
Corned beef brisket	**2 lbs.**	**900 g**
Water	**4 cups**	**1 L**
Bay leaves	**2**	**2**
Whole black peppercorns	**1 tbsp.**	**15 mL**

Layer first 4 ingredients, in order given, in 5 to 7 quart (5 to 7 L) slow cooker. Place corned beef brisket on top, fat-side up.

Add water, bay leaves and peppercorns. Do not stir. Cover. Cook on Low for 8 to 10 hours or on High for 4 to 5 hours. Remove and discard bay leaves. Remove corned beef to large serving platter. Cut into thin slices. Makes 8 servings of meat (2 to 3 oz., 57 to 85 g each, cooked weight). Remove vegetables from slow cooker with slotted spoon to large serving bowl. Serve with corned beef. Serves 8.

1 serving: *251 Calories; 11.5 g Total Fat (5.4 g Mono, 0.5 g Poly, 3.6 g Sat); 61 mg Cholesterol; 20 g Carbohydrate; 3 g Fibre; 18 g Protein; 1757 mg Sodium*

Pictured on page 17.

Make Ahead: The night before, prepare vegetables (except potatoes). Chill overnight in separate covered bowls. Assemble and cook as directed.

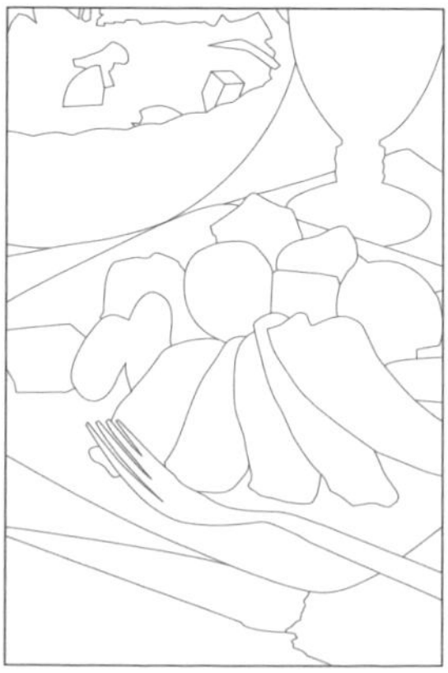

Corned Beef Dinner, above

Props Courtesy Of: Cherison Enterprises Inc.
Danesco Inc.

Sweet Saucy Meatballs

Seasoned meatballs coated in a sweet, tangy cranberry sauce.

Large egg, fork-beaten	1	1
All-bran cereal	3/4 cup	175 mL
Finely chopped onion	1/2 cup	125 mL
Water	1/2 cup	125 mL
Soy sauce	2 tbsp.	30 mL
Garlic powder	1/4 tsp.	1 mL
Salt	1 tsp.	5 mL
Pepper	1/4 tsp.	1 mL
Lean ground beef	1 1/2 lbs.	680 g
Can of whole cranberry sauce	14 oz.	398 mL
Ketchup	1 cup	250 mL
Brown sugar, packed	1/4 cup	60 mL
Lemon juice	1 tbsp.	15 mL

Combine first 8 ingredients in large bowl. Add ground beef. Mix well. Roll mixture into 1 1/2 inch (3.8 cm) balls, using 2 tbsp. (30 mL) for each. Makes about 36 meatballs. Arrange evenly spaced apart on greased baking sheet with sides. Broil 6 inches (15 cm) from heat in oven for about 15 minutes, turning meatballs at halftime, until no longer pink inside.

Measure remaining 4 ingredients into 3 1/2 to 4 quart (3.5 to 4 L) slow cooker. Stir well. Add meatballs. Stir gently. Cover. Cook on Low for 8 to 10 hours or on High for 4 to 5 hours. Serves 6.

1 serving: *488 Calories; 18.4 g Total Fat (7.8 g Mono, 0.9 g Poly, 7.1 g Sat); 100 mg Cholesterol; 60 g Carbohydrate; 5 g Fibre; 25 g Protein; 1436 mg Sodium*

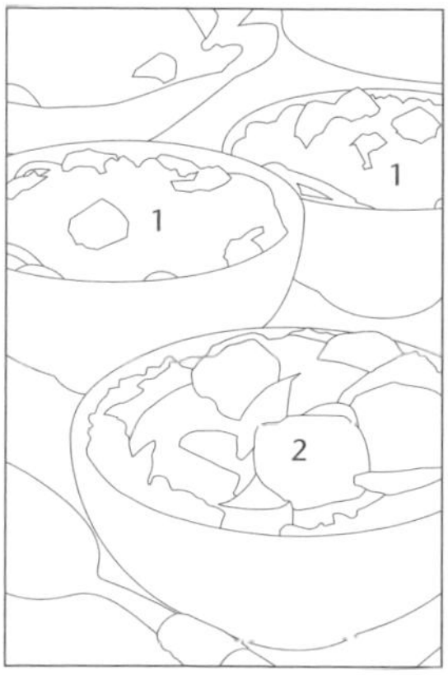

1. Garden Bounty Beef, page 10
2. Meatballs And Snow Peas, page 12

Props Courtesy Of: Anchor Hocking Canada
Casa Bugatti
The Bay

Mexi-Wraps

Tender beef and beans in a thick chili pepper and tomato sauce.

Cooking oil	2 tbsp.	30 mL
Inside round steak, thinly sliced (see Tip, page 87)	2 lbs.	900 g
Water	2 tbsp.	30 mL
All-purpose flour	2 tbsp.	30 mL
Can of white kidney beans, rinsed and drained	19 oz.	540 mL
Can of diced tomatoes, drained	14 oz.	398 mL
Chopped onion	1 cup	250 mL
Chopped green pepper	1 cup	250 mL
Frozen kernel corn	1/2 cup	125 mL
Can of diced green chilies, drained	4 oz.	113 g
Chopped fresh oregano leaves (or 1 1/2 tsp., 7 mL, dried)	2 tbsp.	30 mL
Tomato paste (see Tip, page 13)	2 tbsp.	30 mL
Chili powder	1 tbsp.	15 mL
Garlic cloves, minced (or 1/2 tsp., 2 mL, powder)	2	2
Ground cumin	1 tsp.	5 mL
Salt	1/4 tsp.	1 mL
Grated medium Cheddar cheese	1 cup	250 mL
Flour tortillas (9 inch, 22 cm, diameter)	10	10
Chopped or torn romaine lettuce, lightly packed	1 cup	250 mL

Heat cooking oil in large frying pan on medium-high. Add beef in 2 batches. Cook for 3 to 4 minutes per batch, stirring occasionally, until browned. Transfer to 3 1/2 to 4 quart (3.5 to 4 L) slow cooker.

Stir water into flour in small cup until smooth. Add to beef. Stir.

Add next 12 ingredients. Stir well. Cover. Cook on Low for 7 to 8 hours or on High for 3 1/2 to 4 hours. Makes about 5 cups (1.25 L) filling.

Sprinkle 1 1/2 tbsp. (25 mL) cheese down centre of each tortilla. Spoon 1/2 cup (125 mL) beef mixture onto cheese on each. Divide and scatter lettuce over beef mixture. Fold bottom edge and sides of each tortilla over filling to enclose, leaving top open. Makes 10 wraps.

(continued on next page)

1 wrap: 476 Calories; 19.4 g Total Fat (7.8 g Mono, 2.9 g Poly, 6.6 g Sat); 56 mg Cholesterol; 45 g Carbohydrate; 3 g Fibre; 31 g Protein; 706 mg Sodium

Pictured on page 35.

Make Ahead: The night before, slice steak and prepare bean mixture. Chill overnight in separate covered bowls. Assemble and cook as directed.

Beef Barley Soup

Quick to assemble in the morning—ready when the family arrives in the evening.

Water	**5 cups**	**1.25 L**
Cans of condensed beef broth (10 oz., 284 mL, each)	**2**	**2**
Can of sliced mushrooms, drained	**10 oz.**	**284 mL**
Chopped onion	**1 cup**	**250 mL**
Chopped carrot	**1 cup**	**250 mL**
Can of tomato sauce	**7 1/2 oz.**	**213 mL**
Pearl barley	**1/2 cup**	**125 mL**
Bay leaves	**2**	**2**
Dried thyme	**1 tsp.**	**5 mL**
Salt	**1/4 tsp.**	**1 mL**
Pepper	**1/8 tsp.**	**0.5 mL**
Beef stew meat, cut into 1/2 inch (12 mm) pieces	**1 lb.**	**454 g**
Frozen peas	**1 cup**	**250 mL**
Chopped fresh parsley (or 3/4 tsp., 4 mL, flakes)	**1 tbsp.**	**15 mL**

Combine first 12 ingredients in 4 to 5 quart (4 to 5 L) slow cooker. Cover. Cook on Low for 8 to 10 hours or on High for 4 to 5 hours. Remove and discard bay leaves.

Add peas and parsley. Stir well. Cover. Cook on High for 3 to 5 minutes until peas are heated through. Makes about 12 cups (3 L).

1 cup (250 mL): 132 Calories; 3.7 g Total Fat (1.5 g Mono, 0.3 g Poly, 1.5 g Sat); 21 mg Cholesterol; 13 g Carbohydrate; 2 g Fibre; 12 g Protein; 571 mg Sodium

Pictured on page 90.

Make Ahead: The night before, combine first 11 ingredients in slow cooker liner. Cover. Chill overnight. Cut up beef. Chill overnight in covered bowl. Assemble and cook as directed.

Meatballs In Sauce

Serve over your favourite pasta with garlic toast on the side.

Cans of diced tomatoes (with juice), 19 oz. (540 mL) each	2	2
Chipotle chili pepper, finely chopped (see Tip, page 95)	1	1
Granulated sugar	1 tsp.	5 mL
Bacon slices, cooked almost crisp and chopped	4	4
Fresh bread crumbs	1 cup	250 mL
Finely chopped onion	2/3 cup	150 mL
Chopped fresh parsley (or 1 tbsp., 15 mL, flakes)	1/4 cup	60 mL
Large egg, fork-beaten	1	1
Garlic cloves, minced (or 1/2 tsp., 2 mL, powder)	2	2
Dry mustard	1 tsp.	5 mL
Salt	1/4 tsp.	1 mL
Lean ground beef	1 1/2 lbs.	680 g
Cooking oil	1 tbsp.	15 mL
Sour cream	2 tbsp.	30 mL
Finely chopped fresh parsley, for garnish	1 tbsp.	15 mL

Put tomatoes, chili pepper and sugar into 3 1/2 to 4 quart (3.5 to 4 L) slow cooker. Stir well.

Combine next 8 ingredients in large bowl. Add ground beef. Mix well. Roll mixture into 2 inch (5 cm) balls, using 1/4 cup (60 mL) for each. Makes about 18 meatballs.

Heat cooking oil in large frying pan on medium. Add meatballs in 2 batches. Cook for 8 to 10 minutes per batch, turning occasionally, until browned. Add to tomato mixture. Stir gently. Cover. Cook on Low for 8 to 10 hours or on High for 4 to 5 hours. Remove meatballs with slotted spoon to large serving bowl. Skim and discard any fat from surface of tomato mixture.

Add sour cream to tomato mixture. Stir well. Pour over meatballs. Toss gently. Garnish with second amount of parsley. Serves 6.

(continued on next page)

1 serving: 438 Calories; 24.7 g Total Fat (10.9 g Mono, 2.3 g Poly, 8.7 g Sat); 105 mg Cholesterol; 26 g Carbohydrate; 3 g Fibre; 28 g Protein; 718 mg Sodium

Pictured on page 126.

Make Ahead: The night before, prepare and cook meatballs until no longer pink inside. Drain. Chill overnight in covered bowl. Prepare tomato mixture. Chill overnight in separate covered bowl. Assemble and cook as directed.

Old-Style Chili

Always a favourite, this hearty, chunky chili will fill them up! Serve with warm biscuits.

Chopped onion	**1 cup**	**250 mL**
Diced carrot	**1 cup**	**250 mL**
Chopped green pepper	**1 cup**	**250 mL**
Beef stew meat	**2 lbs.**	**900 g**
Cans of diced tomatoes (with juice), 14 oz. (398 mL) each	**2**	**2**
Can of black beans, rinsed and drained	**19 oz.**	**540 mL**
Can of red kidney beans, rinsed and drained	**14 oz.**	**398 mL**
Can of tomato paste	**5 1/2 oz.**	**156 mL**
Chili powder	**1 – 2 tbsp.**	**15 – 30 mL**
Granulated sugar	**1 tsp.**	**5 mL**
Garlic powder	**1 tsp.**	**5 mL**
Cumin seed	**1 tsp.**	**5 mL**
Caraway seed	**1/2 tsp.**	**2 mL**
Salt	**1/4 tsp.**	**1 mL**

Sour cream, for garnish

Layer first 4 ingredients, in order given, in 4 to 5 quart (4 to 5 L) slow cooker.

Combine next 10 ingredients in large bowl. Pour over beef. Do not stir. Cover. Cook on Low for 8 to 10 hours or on High for 4 to 5 hours.

Garnish individual servings with sour cream. Serves 8.

1 serving: 339 Calories; 10.8 g Total Fat (4.2 g Mono, 0.8 g Poly, 4.1 g Sat); 62 mg Cholesterol; 29 g Carbohydrate; 6 g Fibre; 32 g Protein; 489 mg Sodium

Make Ahead: The night before, chop vegetables and prepare tomato mixture. Chill overnight in separate covered bowls. Assemble and cook as directed.

Red Wine And Rosemary Beef

This rich combination of red wine, rosemary and cranberries will have everyone thinking you've been cooking for hours.

Cooking oil	1 tbsp.	15 mL
Boneless cross-rib roast	3 lbs.	1.4 kg
Cooking oil	1 tbsp.	15 mL
Thinly sliced onion	1 cup	250 mL
Garlic cloves, minced (or 3/4 tsp., 4 mL, powder)	3	3
Dry red (or alcohol-free) wine	1/2 cup	125 mL
Prepared beef broth	1/2 cup	125 mL
Dried cranberries	1/3 cup	75 mL
Sprigs of fresh rosemary	3	3
Salt	1/2 tsp.	2 mL
Pepper	1/2 tsp.	2 mL
Water	2 tbsp.	30 mL
Cornstarch	4 tsp.	20 mL

Heat first amount of cooking oil in large frying pan on medium. Add roast. Cook for 8 to 10 minutes, turning occasionally, until browned on all sides. Transfer to 4 to 5 quart (4 to 5 L) slow cooker.

Heat second amount of cooking oil in same large frying pan on medium. Add onion. Cook for 5 to 10 minutes, stirring often, until softened. Add garlic. Heat and stir for about 1 minute until fragrant. Spread on roast.

Combine next 6 ingredients in same large frying pan. Heat and stir on medium for about 1 minute until hot, scraping any brown bits from bottom of pan. Pour over roast. Cover. Cook on Low for 8 to 10 hours or on High for 4 to 5 hours. Remove and discard rosemary sprigs. Remove roast to large serving platter. Cover to keep warm. Skim and discard any fat from surface of liquid in slow cooker.

Stir water into cornstarch in small cup until smooth. Add to liquid in slow cooker. Stir well. Cover. Cook on High for about 15 minutes until boiling and thickened. Makes about 3 cups (750 mL) sauce. Cut roast into thin slices. Serve with sauce. Makes 12 servings (2 to 3 oz., 57 to 85 g each, cooked weight).

__1 serving:__ 212 Calories; 12.1 g Total Fat (5.5 g Mono, 1.1 g Poly, 4 g Sat); 47 mg Cholesterol; 4 g Carbohydrate; 1 g Fibre; 19 g Protein; 169 mg Sodium

Make Ahead: The night before, slice onion and prepare wine mixture. Chill overnight in separate covered bowls. Assemble and cook as directed.

Slowpoke Cabbage Bake

Savoury mushroom meat sauce tops tender cabbage wedges in this simple but tasty dish.

Large head of savoy (or green) cabbage (about 1 3/4 lbs., 790 g), cut into 8 wedges	1	1
Bacon slices	6	6
Lean ground beef	1 lb.	454 g
Chopped onion	1/2 cup	125 mL
Garlic clove, minced (or 1/4 tsp., 1 mL, powder)	1	1
Can of condensed cream of mushroom soup	10 oz.	284 mL
Can of mushroom stems and pieces (with liquid)	10 oz.	284 mL
Prepared beef broth	1/2 cup	125 mL
Tomato paste (see Tip, page 13)	3 tbsp.	50 mL
Dried thyme	1/2 tsp.	2 mL
Dried whole oregano	1/4 tsp.	1 mL
Salt	1/2 tsp.	2 mL

Put cabbage wedges, rounded-side up, into 4 to 5 quart (4 to 5 L) slow cooker.

Cook bacon in large frying pan on medium until crisp. Remove to paper towels to drain. Crumble. Set aside. Remove and discard drippings, reserving 1 tbsp. (15 mL) in pan.

Heat reserved drippings in same large frying pan on medium. Add ground beef, onion and garlic. Scramble-fry for 5 to 10 minutes until beef is no longer pink. Drain.

Add bacon and remaining 7 ingredients. Stir well. Pour over cabbage. Do not stir. Cover. Cook on Low for 8 to 10 hours or on High for 4 to 5 hours. Serves 8.

***1 serving:** 241 Calories; 14 g Total Fat (5.4 g Mono, 2.1 g Poly, 5.1 g Sat); 36 mg Cholesterol; 14 g Carbohydrate; 5 g Fibre; 16 g Protein; 735 mg Sodium*

Make Ahead: The night before, put cabbage wedges into slow cooker liner. Cover. Chill overnight. Prepare bacon and ground beef mixture as directed. Chill overnight in covered bowl. Prepare mushroom soup mixture. Chill overnight in separate covered bowl. Assemble and cook as directed.

Beef In Beer

Tender beef in a rich, slightly sweet sauce tops thick French bread slices seasoned with Dijon mustard.

Cooking oil	**2 tsp.**	**10 mL**
Chopped onion	**1 cup**	**250 mL**
Bacon slices, diced	**6**	**6**
All-purpose flour	**3 tbsp.**	**50 mL**
Beef stew meat	**2 lbs.**	**900 g**
Cooking oil	**2 tbsp.**	**30 mL**
Can of beer (see Note)	**12 1/2 oz.**	**355 mL**
Dijon mustard	**1 tbsp.**	**15 mL**
Granulated sugar	**2 tsp.**	**10 mL**
Dried thyme	**1 tsp.**	**5 mL**
French bread slices (about 1 inch, 2.5 cm, thick), toasted	**8**	**8**
Dijon mustard	**2 1/2 tbsp.**	**37 mL**

Heat first amount of cooking oil in large frying pan on medium. Add onion and bacon. Cook for 5 to 10 minutes, stirring often, until onion is softened. Transfer with slotted spoon to 3 1/2 to 4 quart (3.5 to 4 L) slow cooker. Discard drippings.

Measure flour into large resealable freezer bag. Add 1/2 of beef. Seal bag. Toss until coated. Repeat with remaining beef. Heat second amount of cooking oil in same large frying pan on medium. Add beef in 2 batches. Cook for 5 to 10 minutes per batch, stirring occasionally, until browned.

Combine next 4 ingredients in 2 cup (500 mL) liquid measure. Slowly add to beef, stirring constantly and scraping any brown bits from bottom of pan, until boiling. Add to onion mixture. Stir well. Cover. Cook on Low for 8 to 9 hours or on High for 4 to 4 1/2 hours.

Place 1 bread slice on each of 8 plates. Spread about 1 tsp. (5 mL) mustard on each bread slice. Spoon 1/2 cup (125 mL) beef mixture on top of each slice. Serves 8.

1 serving: *405 Calories; 18.3 g Total Fat (8.5 g Mono, 2.6 g Poly, 5.4 g Sat); 66 mg Cholesterol; 25 g Carbohydrate; 1 g Fibre; 30 g Protein; 461 mg Sodium*

Note: For best results, use brown ale for its smooth, slightly sweet flavour.

Cabbage Rouladen

These savoury beef rolls are hard to resist.
They take a little bit longer to prepare, but are well worth the time.

Shredded cabbage, lightly packed	**3 cups**	**750 mL**
Dijon mustard	**1/3 cup**	**75 mL**
Creamed horseradish	**2 tbsp.**	**30 mL**
Pepper	**1/2 tsp.**	**2 mL**
Rouladen steaks (about 4 oz., 113 g, each), 1/4 inch (6 mm) thick	**6**	**6**
Bacon slices, halved	**3**	**3**
Finely chopped onion	**1/2 cup**	**125 mL**
Large dill pickles, halved lengthwise	**3**	**3**
Can of condensed cream of mushroom soup	**10 oz.**	**284 mL**
Prepared beef broth	**1/2 cup**	**125 mL**
Dijon mustard	**2 tbsp.**	**30 mL**

Put cabbage into 4 to 5 quart (4 to 5 L) slow cooker.

Combine first amount of mustard, horseradish and pepper in small bowl. Divide and spread evenly on 1 side of each steak.

Lay 1 bacon strip crosswise on top of mustard mixture in centre of each steak. Divide and sprinkle onion over bacon on each. Place 1 pickle half crosswise near short end of each steak. Roll up, jelly roll-style, from short end to enclose filling. Secure each roll with wooden pick. Arrange rolls, criss-crossed in 2 layers, on top of cabbage.

Combine remaining 3 ingredients in medium bowl. Pour over rolls. Do not stir. Cover. Cook on Low for 8 to 10 hours or on High for 4 to 5 hours. Transfer rolls with slotted spoon to large plate. Remove and discard wooden picks. Remove cabbage with slotted spoon to large serving platter. Arrange rolls, seam-side down, on top of cabbage. Drizzle sauce from slow cooker over individual servings. Serves 6.

1 serving: *339 Calories; 20.3 g Total Fat (8.7 g Mono, 4 g Poly, 8.5 g Sat); 56 mg Cholesterol; 10 g Carbohydrate; 2 g Fibre; 29 g Protein; 1302 mg Sodium*

Apple And Beef Pot Roast

Ginger and apples add an appealing aroma to this comforting meal. Serve with mashed potatoes and roasted vegetables.

Boneless blade (or chuck) roast	3 lbs.	1.4 kg
Whole cloves	6	6
Salt	1/2 tsp.	2 mL
Pepper	1/2 tsp.	2 mL
Cooking oil	1 tbsp.	15 mL
Tart medium cooking apples (such as Granny Smith), peeled and cores removed, cut into 1/2 inch (12 mm) slices	4	4
Thinly sliced onion	1 cup	250 mL
Apple juice	1/2 cup	125 mL
Prepared beef broth	1/4 cup	60 mL
Ground ginger	3/4 tsp.	4 mL
Water	3 tbsp.	50 mL
All-purpose flour	1 tbsp.	15 mL

Cut 6 shallow slits in roast at random. Insert 1 clove into each slit. Sprinkle roast with salt and pepper.

Heat cooking oil in large frying pan on medium-high. Add roast. Cook for 5 to 10 minutes, turning often, until browned on all sides. Transfer to 4 to 5 quart (4 to 5 L) slow cooker.

Scatter apple and onion over top of roast.

Combine apple juice, broth and ginger in small bowl. Pour over roast. Cover. Cook on Low for 8 to 10 hours or on High for 4 to 5 hours. Remove roast to large serving platter. Remove and discard cloves. Cover to keep warm.

Stir water into flour in small cup until smooth. Add to liquid in slow cooker. Stir well. Cover. Cook on High for about 15 minutes until thickened. Carefully process with hand blender or in blender until smooth. Makes about 4 1/2 cups (1.1 L) sauce. Cut roast into thin slices. Serve with sauce. Makes 12 servings (2 to 3 oz., 57 to 85 g each, cooked weight).

1 serving: *287 Calories; 18.2 g Total Fat (8.1 g Mono, 1 g Poly, 6.9 g Sat); 67 mg Cholesterol; 9 g Carbohydrate; 1 g Fibre; 21 g Protein; 194 mg Sodium*

Make Ahead: The night before, slice onion and prepare apple juice mixture. Chill overnight in separate covered bowls. Assemble and cook as directed.

Shredded Beef On A Bun

The perfect meal for a casual crowd. Serve with coleslaw, potato salad, a variety of pickles—and let the party begin!

Sliced onion	**1 cup**	**250 mL**
Prepared chicken broth	**1 cup**	**250 mL**
Red wine vinegar	**1/2 cup**	**125 mL**
Brown sugar, packed	**1/2 cup**	**125 mL**
Tomato paste (see Tip, page 13)	**1/4 cup**	**60 mL**
Soy sauce	**2 tbsp.**	**30 mL**
Prepared mustard	**2 tbsp.**	**30 mL**
Garlic cloves, minced (or 1 tsp., 5 mL, powder)	**4**	**4**
Salt	**1/2 tsp.**	**2 mL**
Boneless blade (or chuck) roast	**3 lbs.**	**1.4 kg**
Kaiser rolls (or your favourite), split	**12**	**12**

Combine first 9 ingredients in 3 1/2 to 4 quart (3.5 to 4 L) slow cooker.

Add roast. Turn until coated. Cover. Cook on Low for 8 to 10 hours or on High for 4 to 5 hours. Transfer roast to large plate. Cover to keep warm. Skim and discard any fat from surface of liquid in slow cooker. Strain liquid through sieve into large frying pan. Transfer solids to small bowl. Set aside. Bring liquid to a boil on medium-high. Boil gently for about 15 minutes, stirring occasionally, until sauce is thickened and reduced by almost half. Makes about 1 3/4 cups (425 mL) sauce. Shred beef with 2 forks. Add to sauce. Add reserved solids. Stir well. Makes about 5 cups (1.25 L) shredded beef mixture.

Divide and spoon beef mixture onto bottom half of each roll. Cover each with top half of roll. Makes 12 beef buns.

1 beef bun: *397 Calories; 10.4 g Total Fat (3.6 g Mono, 1.5 g Poly, 3.2 g Sat); 55 mg Cholesterol; 43 g Carbohydrate; 2 g Fibre; 31 g Protein; 766 mg Sodium*

Make Ahead: The night before, assemble first 9 ingredients, as directed, in slow cooker liner. Cover. Chill overnight. Add roast. Cook as directed.

Paré Pointer

He says the only reason he is in prison is because they keep the door locked.

Beef And Apricot Braise

Cumin, coriander and apricot add a subtly sweet, exotic flavour to tender beef. Serve with oven-roasted potatoes and steamed vegetables.

Chopped carrot	**1 cup**	**250 mL**
All-purpose flour	**3 tbsp.**	**50 mL**
Beef stew meat	**2 lbs.**	**900 g**
Cooking oil	**2 tbsp.**	**30 mL**
Cooking oil	**2 tsp.**	**10 mL**
Chopped onion	**1 1/2 cups**	**375 mL**
Garlic cloves, minced (or 1/2 tsp., 2 mL, powder)	**2**	**2**
Ground cumin	**1/2 tsp.**	**2 mL**
Ground coriander	**1/2 tsp.**	**2 mL**
Chopped dried apricot	**1 cup**	**250 mL**
Prepared beef broth	**1 cup**	**250 mL**
Dry sherry (or apple juice)	**1/2 cup**	**125 mL**
Bay leaf	**1**	**1**
Salt	**1/4 tsp.**	**1 mL**
Pepper	**1/4 tsp.**	**1 mL**
Chopped fresh (or frozen, thawed) green beans	**1 cup**	**250 mL**

Scatter carrot in bottom of 3 1/2 to 4 quart (3.5 to 4 L) slow cooker.

Measure flour into large resealable freezer bag. Add 1/2 of beef. Seal bag. Toss until coated. Repeat with remaining beef. Heat first amount of cooking oil in large frying pan on medium. Add beef in 2 batches. Cook for 5 to 10 minutes per batch, stirring occasionally, until browned. Layer on top of carrot.

Heat second amount of cooking oil in same large frying pan on medium. Add onion. Cook for 5 to 10 minutes, stirring often and scraping any brown bits from bottom of pan, until softened.

Add next 3 ingredients. Heat and stir for about 1 minute until fragrant. Spread on top of beef.

Combine next 6 ingredients in medium bowl. Pour over beef mixture. Do not stir. Cover. Cook on Low for 8 to 10 hours or on High for 4 to 5 hours.

(continued on next page)

Add green beans. Stir well. Cover. Cook on High for 10 to 15 minutes until beans are tender-crisp. Remove and discard bay leaf. Serves 8.

__1 serving:__ 315 Calories; 13.5 g Total Fat (6.3 g Mono, 1.5 g Poly, 4.2 g Sat); 62 mg Cholesterol; 20 g Carbohydrate; 3 g Fibre; 27 g Protein; 262 mg Sodium

Make Ahead: The night before, chop vegetables and prepare apricot mixture. Chill overnight in separate covered bowls. Assemble and cook as directed.

Sloppy Joes

An old favourite—quick to put together and easy to serve. The perfect answer for dinner on busy evenings!

Cooking oil	**2 tsp.**	**10 mL**
Lean ground beef	**2 lbs.**	**900 g**
Can of tomato sauce	**14 oz.**	**398 mL**
Chopped onion	**1 1/2 cups**	**375 mL**
Thinly sliced celery	**1 cup**	**250 mL**
Barbecue sauce	**2 tbsp.**	**30 mL**
Worcestershire sauce	**2 tsp.**	**10 mL**
Salt, sprinkle		
Pepper (optional)	**1/4 tsp.**	**1 mL**
Grated medium Cheddar cheese	**1 1/2 cups**	**375 mL**
Kaiser rolls, split (toasted, optional)	**8**	**8**

Heat cooking oil in large frying pan on medium. Add ground beef. Scramble-fry for 5 to 10 minutes until no longer pink. Drain. Transfer to 3 1/2 to 4 quart (3.5 to 4 L) slow cooker.

Add next 7 ingredients. Stir well. Cover. Cook on Low for 8 to 9 hours or on High for 4 to 4 1/2 hours.

Add cheese. Stir until melted. Makes about 4 cups (1 L) beef mixture. Place 1 bottom half of rolls on each of 8 plates. Divide and spoon beef mixture onto bottom half. Cover with top half of roll on each. Serves 8.

__1 serving:__ 471 Calories; 20.6 g Total Fat (7.6 g Mono, 2 g Poly, 8.9 g Sat); 82 mg Cholesterol; 38 g Carbohydrate; 3 g Fibre; 33 g Protein; 866 mg Sodium

Pictured on page 35.

Make Ahead: The night before, prepare tomato sauce mixture. Chill overnight in covered bowl. Scramble-fry beef until no longer pink. Drain. Chill overnight in separate covered bowl. Assemble and cook as directed.

Tomato Meat Sauce

Dried crushed chilies make this thick, spicy sauce just a little different. Serve over your favourite pasta.

Cooking oil	1 tbsp.	15 mL
Lean ground beef	2 lbs.	900 g
Cooking oil	2 tsp.	10 mL
Finely chopped onion	2 cups	500 mL
Sliced fresh white mushrooms	2 cups	500 mL
Garlic cloves, minced	4	4
Can of diced tomatoes (with juice)	28 oz.	796 mL
Can of tomato paste	5 1/2 oz.	156 mL
Chopped fresh oregano leaves (or 1 1/2 tsp., 7 mL, dried)	2 tbsp.	30 mL
Bay leaf	1	1
Granulated sugar	1 tsp.	5 mL
Dried crushed chilies	1/2 tsp.	2 mL
Salt	1/4 tsp.	1 mL
Pepper	1/2 tsp.	2 mL
Chopped fresh basil (see Note), optional	2 tbsp.	30 mL

Heat first amount of cooking oil in large frying pan on medium. Add ground beef. Scramble-fry for 5 to 10 minutes until no longer pink. Drain. Transfer to 3 1/2 to 4 quart (3.5 to 4 L) slow cooker.

Heat second amount of cooking oil in same large frying pan on medium. Add onion. Cook for 5 to 10 minutes, stirring often, until softened.

Add mushrooms and garlic. Cook for about 5 minutes, stirring occasionally, until mushrooms are lightly browned. Add to beef. Stir.

Add next 8 ingredients. Stir well. Cover. Cook on Low for 8 to 10 hours or on High for 4 to 5 hours. Remove and discard bay leaf.

Add basil. Stir well. Serves 8.

__1 serving:__ 323 Calories; 19.3 g Total Fat (8.5 g Mono, 1.5 g Poly, 7 g Sat); 63 mg Cholesterol; 14 g Carbohydrate; 3 g Fibre; 24 g Protein; 331 mg Sodium

Note: Omit fresh basil. Add 1 1/2 tsp. (7 mL) dried basil to tomato mixture before adding to beef mixture.

(continued on next page)

Make Ahead: The night before, prepare tomato mixture. Chill overnight in covered bowl. Scramble-fry ground beef until no longer pink. Drain. Chill overnight in separate covered bowl. Assemble and cook as directed.

Beef Stew Diane

A less peppery cousin of Hungarian goulash, with a unique brandy accent. Serve over egg noodles with a salad on the side.

All-purpose flour	**3 tbsp.**	**50 mL**
Pepper	**1/2 tsp.**	**2 mL**
Beef stew meat	**2 lbs.**	**900 g**
Cooking oil	**2 tbsp.**	**30 mL**
Cooking oil	**2 tsp.**	**10 mL**
Chopped onion	**1 1/2 cups**	**375 mL**
Can of diced tomatoes (with juice)	**14 oz.**	**398 mL**
Prepared beef broth	**1 cup**	**250 mL**
Worcestershire sauce	**2 tbsp.**	**30 mL**
Sour cream	**1/4 cup**	**60 mL**
Brandy (or apple juice)	**2 – 3 tbsp.**	**30 – 50 mL**
Chopped fresh parsley (or 1 1/2 tsp., 7 mL, dried)	**2 tbsp.**	**30 mL**

Combine flour and pepper in large resealable freezer bag. Add 1/2 of beef. Seal bag. Toss until coated. Repeat with remaining beef. Heat first amount of cooking oil in large frying pan on medium. Add beef in 2 batches. Cook for 5 to 10 minutes per batch, stirring occasionally, until browned. Transfer to 3 1/2 to 4 quart (3.5 to 4 L) slow cooker.

Heat second amount of cooking oil in same large frying pan on medium. Add onion. Cook for 5 to 10 minutes, stirring often, until softened. Add to beef. Stir.

Add next 3 ingredients to beef mixture. Stir well. Cover. Cook on Low for 8 to 9 hours or on High for 4 to 4 1/2 hours.

Add remaining 3 ingredients. Stir well. Serves 8.

1 serving: *290 Calories; 15.6 g Total Fat (7.2 g Mono, 1.9 g Poly, 5 g Sat); 65 mg Cholesterol; 8 g Carbohydrate; 1 g Fibre; 26 g Protein; 303 mg Sodium*

Make Ahead: The night before, chop onion and prepare tomato mixture. Chill overnight in separate covered bowls. Assemble and cook as directed.

Tomato Olive Beef

Rich flavours abound in this mildly spiced dish. Serve with rice.

Can of diced tomatoes (with juice)	**28 oz.**	**796 mL**
Thinly sliced red onion	**1 1/2 cups**	**375 mL**
Fresh chilies, seeds and ribs removed (see Tip, page 95), chopped	**2**	**2**
Tomato paste (see Tip, page 13)	**1/3 cup**	**75 mL**
Dry red (or alcohol-free) wine	**1/4 cup**	**60 mL**
Chili powder	**1 tbsp.**	**15 mL**
Salt	**1/4 tsp.**	**1 mL**
Pepper	**1/4 tsp.**	**1 mL**
Beef stew meat	**2 lbs.**	**900 g**
Bacon slices, cooked crisp and crumbled	**6**	**6**
Chopped fresh basil (see Note)	**1/4 cup**	**60 mL**
Kalamata olives (Greek), pitted and chopped	**6**	**6**
Pine nuts, toasted (see Tip, page 39), for garnish (optional)	**1/4 cup**	**60 mL**

Combine first 8 ingredients in 3 1/2 to 4 quart (3.5 to 4 L) slow cooker. Add beef and bacon. Stir well. Cover. Cook on Low for 8 to 10 hours or on High for 4 to 5 hours.

Add basil. Stir well. Remove to large serving bowl. Scatter olives and pine nuts over top. Serves 8.

***1 serving:** 279 Calories; 13 g Total Fat (5.6 g Mono, 0.9 g Poly, 4.9 g Sat); 66 mg Cholesterol; 11 g Carbohydrate; 2 g Fibre; 28 g Protein; 456 mg Sodium*

Note: Omit fresh basil. Add 1 tbsp. (15 mL) dried basil to first 10 ingredients.

1. Mexi-Wraps, page 20
2. Sloppy Joes, page 31

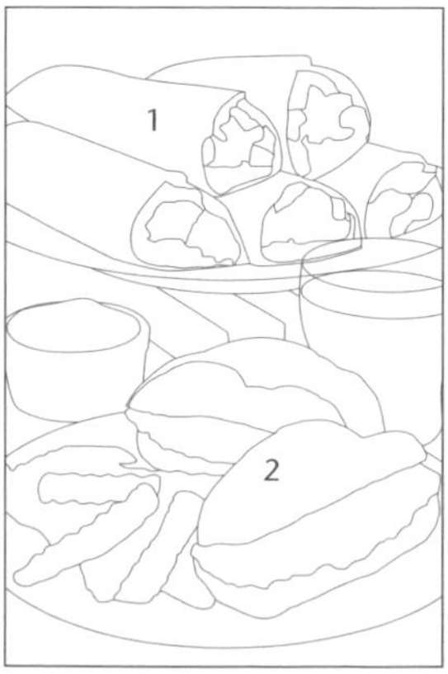

Lemon Cream Chicken

Scrumptious served over buttered noodles.

Cooking oil	1 tbsp.	15 mL
Boneless, skinless chicken thighs (about 12)	1 1/2 lbs.	680 g
Chopped onion	1 cup	250 mL
Chopped carrot	2 cups	500 mL
Chopped celery	1 cup	250 mL
Sliced fresh white mushrooms	2 cups	500 mL
Prepared chicken broth	1 cup	250 mL
Italian seasoning	1 tsp.	5 mL
Salt	1/4 tsp.	1 mL
Pepper	1/4 tsp.	1 mL
Water	1 tbsp.	15 mL
Cornstarch	1 tbsp.	15 mL
Sour cream	1/4 cup	60 mL
Lemon juice	1 tbsp.	15 mL

Heat cooking oil in large frying pan on medium. Add chicken. Cook for 5 to 10 minutes, turning occasionally, until browned.

Layer next 4 ingredients, in order given, in 3 1/2 to 4 quart (3.5 to 4 L) slow cooker. Arrange chicken over vegetables. Combine next 4 ingredients in small bowl. Pour over chicken. Do not stir. Cover. Cook on Low for 8 to 10 hours or on High for 4 to 5 hours.

Stir water into cornstarch in small bowl until smooth. Add sour cream and lemon juice. Stir. Add to chicken mixture. Stir. Cover. Cook on High for about 5 minutes until sauce is thickened. Serves 6.

***1 serving:** 258 Calories; 11 g Total Fat (4 g Mono, 2.6 g Poly, 2.9 g Sat); 107 mg Cholesterol; 13 g Carbohydrate; 3 g Fibre; 27 g Protein; 361 mg Sodium*

1. Country Chicken Stew, page 47
2. Ginger Beef Stew, page 14

Props Courtesy Of: Danesco Inc.
The Bay

Apple Chicken Dinner

A complete meal, perfect for company or a relaxing family dinner. Don't let the long list of ingredients keep you from trying this delicious combination that's easy to prepare the night before.

APPLE ALMOND STUFFING		
Hard margarine (or butter)	1/4 cup	60 mL
Finely chopped onion	1/2 cup	125 mL
Finely chopped celery	1/2 cup	125 mL
Slivered almonds	1/2 cup	125 mL
Tart medium cooking apple (such as Granny Smith), peeled and core removed, diced	1	1
Coarse dry bread crumbs (or cubes)	1 1/2 cups	375 mL
Parsley flakes	2 tsp.	10 mL
Ground sage	1/4 tsp.	1 mL
Dried thyme	1/4 tsp.	1 mL
Salt	1/4 tsp.	1 mL
Pepper	1/8 tsp.	0.5 mL
Prepared chicken broth	1/2 cup	125 mL
Coarsely chopped onion	1 cup	250 mL
Baby carrots	9 oz.	255 g
Halved fresh (or frozen, thawed) green beans	2 cups	500 mL
Tart medium cooking apple (such as Granny Smith), peeled and core removed, cut into 8 wedges	1	1
Cooking oil	1 tbsp.	15 mL
Boneless, skinless chicken thighs (2 – 3 oz., 57 – 85 g, each)	12	12
Prepared chicken broth	1/2 cup	125 mL
Apple (or orange) juice	1/2 cup	125 mL
Dry sherry (or apple juice)	1/3 cup	75 mL
Salt	1/4 tsp.	1 mL
Water	1 tbsp.	15 mL
Cornstarch	1 tbsp.	15 mL

(continued on next page)

Apple Almond Stuffing: Melt margarine in large frying pan on medium. Add first amount of onion, celery and almonds. Cook for 5 to 10 minutes, stirring often, until onion is softened and almonds are browned. Remove from heat.

Add next 7 ingredients. Stir.

Slowly add first amount of broth, stirring constantly until just moistened. Stuffing will still be quite dry. Makes about 3 cups (750 mL) stuffing. Spoon stuffing onto centre of 12 inch (30 cm) sheet of parchment (not waxed) paper or foil. Fold sides over stuffing. Roll up from bottom to enclose stuffing. Set aside.

Layer next 4 ingredients, in order given, in 4 to 5 quart (4 to 5 L) slow cooker.

Heat cooking oil in same large frying pan on medium. Add chicken. Cook for 8 to 10 minutes, turning occasionally, until browned. Arrange on top of apple wedges.

Combine next 4 ingredients in small bowl. Pour over chicken. Do not stir. Place stuffing packet, seam-side down, on top of chicken. Cover. Cook on Low for 7 to 8 hours or on High for 3 1/2 to 4 hours. Carefully remove stuffing packet. Remove stuffing to centre of large serving platter. Discard parchment paper. Remove chicken and vegetables with slotted spoon to same large serving platter, arranging around stuffing. Cover to keep warm.

Stir water into cornstarch in small cup until smooth. Add to liquid in slow cooker. Stir well. Cover. Cook on High for about 15 minutes until slightly thickened. Makes about 1 cup (250 mL) sauce. Serve with chicken and vegetables. Serves 6.

***1 serving:** 526 Calories; 24.7 g Total Fat (13.1 g Mono, 4.9 g Poly, 4.5 g Sat); 94 mg Cholesterol; 45 g Carbohydrate; 5 g Fibre; 30 g Protein; 706 mg Sodium*

Make Ahead: The night before, prepare stuffing and enclose in parchment paper. Chill overnight. Prepare vegetables. Chill overnight in separate covered bowls. Assemble and cook as directed.

tip *To toast nuts or seeds, spread evenly in ungreased shallow pan. Bake in 350°F (175°C) oven for 5 to 10 minutes, stirring or shaking often, until desired doneness.*

Coq Au Vin

Sounds fancy, tastes like it too, but it's easy to prepare this delicious French stew! "Coq" is chicken, "vin" is wine—supper's ready—come, let's dine!

Bacon slices, diced	**6**	**6**
All-purpose flour	**1/4 cup**	**60 mL**
Paprika	**1/4 tsp.**	**1 mL**
Boneless, skinless chicken thighs (2 – 3 oz., 57 – 85 g, each)	**12**	**12**
Halved fresh white mushrooms	**4 cups**	**1 L**
Chopped onion	**1 cup**	**250 mL**
Garlic clove, minced (or 1/4 tsp., 1 mL, powder)	**1**	**1**
Can of condensed cream of mushroom soup	**10 oz.**	**284 mL**
Prepared chicken broth	**1/2 cup**	**125 mL**
Dry red (or alcohol-free) wine	**1/2 cup**	**125 mL**
Dried thyme	**1/2 tsp.**	**2 mL**
Bay leaves	**2**	**2**
Chopped fresh parsley, for garnish	**2 tbsp.**	**30 mL**

Cook bacon in large frying pan on medium until crisp. Remove to paper towels to drain. Remove and discard drippings, reserving 1 tbsp. (15 mL) in pan. Set aside.

Combine flour and paprika in large resealable freezer bag. Add 1/2 of chicken. Seal bag. Toss until coated. Repeat with remaining chicken. Heat reserved drippings in same large frying pan on medium. Add chicken in 2 batches. Cook for 8 to 10 minutes per batch, turning occasionally, until browned. Transfer to 3 1/2 to 4 quart (3.5 to 4 L) slow cooker.

Add mushrooms, onion and garlic to same large frying pan. Cook for about 2 minutes, stirring occasionally and scraping any brown bits from bottom of pan, until onion starts to soften.

Add bacon and next 5 ingredients. Heat and stir for about 2 minutes until mixture just starts to boil. Pour over chicken. Cover. Cook on Low for 7 to 8 hours or on High for 3 1/2 to 4 hours. Remove and discard bay leaves. Remove chicken mixture to large serving platter.

(continued on next page)

Garnish with parsley. Serves 6.

1 serving: 318 Calories; 15.7 g Total Fat (5.2 g Mono, 4.1 g Poly, 4.7 g Sat); 102 mg Cholesterol; 13 g Carbohydrate; 1 g Fibre; 27 g Protein; 580 mg Sodium

Make Ahead: The night before, prepare mushrooms and onion. Chill overnight in separate covered bowls. Prepare mushroom soup mixture. Chill overnight in separate covered bowl. Assemble and cook as directed.

Cajun Chicken And Rice

A colourful concoction with a cheeky Cajun kick!

Can of red kidney beans, rinsed and drained	**19 oz.**	**540 mL**
Sliced red pepper	**1 1/2 cups**	**375 mL**
Frozen kernel corn	**1 cup**	**250 mL**
Prepared chicken broth	**1 cup**	**250 mL**
Cajun seasoning	**1 tbsp.**	**15 mL**
Ground cumin	**1 tsp.**	**5 mL**
Boneless, skinless chicken thighs, chopped	**1 lb.**	**454 g**
Can of diced tomatoes (with juice)	**14 oz.**	**398 mL**
Long grain white rice	**1/2 cup**	**125 mL**
Sliced zucchini (with peel)	**1 cup**	**250 mL**
Chopped fresh cilantro or parsley (or 1 1/2 tsp., 7 mL, dried)	**2 tbsp.**	**30 mL**

Combine first 7 ingredients in 3 1/2 to 4 quart (3.5 to 4 L) slow cooker. Cover. Cook on Low for 8 to 10 hours or on High for 4 to 5 hours.

Add tomatoes and rice. Stir gently. Cover. Cook on High for 30 to 40 minutes until rice is almost tender.

Add zucchini and cilantro. Stir gently. Cover. Cook on High for 10 to 15 minutes until rice and zucchini are tender. Serves 4.

1 serving: 416 Calories; 8.2 g Total Fat (2.3 g Mono, 2.2 g Poly, 1.9 g Sat); 94 mg Cholesterol; 54 g Carbohydrate; 8 g Fibre; 34 g Protein; 547 mg Sodium

Make Ahead: The night before, combine first 6 ingredients in slow cooker liner. Cover. Chill overnight. Add chicken the next morning. Cook as directed.

Snappy Pineapple Chicken

Sweet bites of pineapple with a lively snap from ginger and lemon pepper. Saucy! Serve over jasmine or coconut rice.

Large onion, cut into 8 wedges	1	1
Baby carrots	12 oz.	340 g
All-purpose flour	1/4 cup	60 mL
Paprika	2 1/2 tsp.	12 mL
Lemon pepper	2 1/2 tsp.	12 mL
Ground ginger	2 1/2 tsp.	12 mL
Boneless, skinless chicken breast halves (4 – 6 oz., 113 – 170 g, each), each cut into 2 pieces	6	6
Boneless, skinless chicken thighs (2 – 3 oz., 57 – 85 g, each)	12	12
Prepared chicken broth	1 cup	250 mL
Reserved pineapple juice	1/2 cup	125 mL
Soy sauce	2 tbsp.	30 mL
Brown sugar, packed	2 tbsp.	30 mL
Chili sauce	2 tbsp.	30 mL
Ground allspice	1/4 tsp.	1 mL
Large red pepper, seeds and ribs removed, cut into 1 inch (2.5 cm) pieces	1	1
Can of pineapple tidbits, drained and juice reserved	14 oz.	398 mL
Can of sliced water chestnuts, drained	8 oz.	227 mL
Water	2 tbsp.	30 mL
Cornstarch	2 tbsp.	30 mL

Put onion and carrots into 4 to 5 quart (4 to 5 L) slow cooker.

Combine next 4 ingredients in large resealable freezer bag. Add 1/3 of chicken breast pieces and thighs. Seal bag. Toss until coated. Repeat twice with remaining 2/3 of chicken. Arrange chicken on top of carrots.

Combine next 6 ingredients in 2 cup (500 mL) liquid measure. Pour over chicken. Do not stir. Cover. Cook on Low for 8 to 9 hours or on High for 4 to 4 1/2 hours.

(continued on next page)

Add red pepper, pineapple and water chestnuts. Stir.

Stir water into cornstarch in small cup until smooth. Add to chicken mixture. Stir well. Cover. Cook on High for about 20 minutes until red pepper is tender-crisp and sauce is slightly thickened. Serves 12.

__1 serving:__ 224 Calories; 4.4 g Total Fat (1.3 g Mono, 1.1 g Poly, 1.1 g Sat); 80 mg Cholesterol; 20 g Carbohydrate; 2 g Fibre; 26 g Protein; 542 mg Sodium

Pictured on page 72 and on back cover.

Make Ahead: The night before, cut up vegetables and prepare broth mixture. Chill overnight in separate covered bowls. Assemble and cook as directed.

Creamy Chicken Dijon

A cheesy chicken stew, brimming with broccoli.

Chopped onion	**1 1/2 cups**	**375 mL**
Can of sliced mushrooms, drained	**10 oz.**	**284 mL**
Can of condensed cream of chicken soup	**10 oz.**	**284 mL**
Water	**1/2 cup**	**125 mL**
Dijon mustard	**1/4 cup**	**60 mL**
Dried crushed chilies	**1/4 tsp.**	**1 mL**
Boneless, skinless chicken breast halves (4 – 6 oz., 113 – 170 g, each), each cut into 2 pieces	**8**	**8**
Can of evaporated milk	**5 1/2 oz.**	**160 mL**
Bag of frozen cut broccoli, thawed, chopped smaller	**26 oz.**	**750 g**

Combine first 6 ingredients in 4 to 5 quart (4 to 5 L) slow cooker.

Add chicken. Stir well. Cover. Cook on Low for 8 to 9 hours or on High for 4 to 4 1/2 hours.

Add evaporated milk. Stir. Add broccoli. Stir well. Cover. Cook on High for about 20 minutes until heated through and broccoli is tender-crisp. Serves 8.

__1 serving:__ 237 Calories; 6.7 g Total Fat (2.1 g Mono, 1.4 g Poly, 2.3 g Sat); 75 mg Cholesterol; 14 g Carbohydrate; 3 g Fibre; 32 g Protein; 525 mg Sodium

Make Ahead: The night before, combine first 6 ingredients in slow cooker liner. Cover. Chill overnight. Add chicken. Cook as directed.

Pesto Chicken Pasta

Light, mildly spiced sauce coats pasta, red pepper and chicken.

Chopped red onion	**1 cup**	**250 mL**
Dry white (or alcohol-free) wine	**1 cup**	**250 mL**
Red medium peppers, seeds and ribs removed, cut into strips	**2**	**2**
Garlic cloves, minced (or 1/2 tsp., 2 mL, powder)	**2**	**2**
Chili powder	**1 tsp.**	**5 mL**
Salt	**1/2 tsp.**	**2 mL**
Pepper	**1/2 tsp.**	**2 mL**
Boneless, skinless chicken thighs (2 – 3 oz., 57 – 85 g, each), halved	**12**	**12**
Lemon juice	**1 tbsp.**	**15 mL**
Cornstarch	**1 tbsp.**	**15 mL**
Sun-dried tomato pesto	**3 tbsp.**	**50 mL**
Penne pasta (about 10 oz., 285 g)	**3 cups**	**750 mL**
Boiling water	**12 cups**	**3 L**
Salt	**1 1/2 tsp.**	**7 mL**
Grated Parmesan cheese	**1/3 cup**	**75 mL**

Combine first 7 ingredients in 3 1/2 to 4 quart (3.5 to 4 L) slow cooker. Add chicken. Stir well. Cover. Cook on Low for 7 to 8 hours or on High for 3 1/2 to 4 hours.

Stir lemon juice into cornstarch in small cup until smooth. Add pesto. Stir well. Add to chicken mixture. Stir. Cover. Cook on High for about 15 minutes until sauce is thickened.

Cook pasta in boiling water and second amount of salt in large uncovered pot or Dutch oven for about 15 minutes, stirring occasionally, until tender but firm. Drain. Return pasta to pot. Add chicken mixture. Toss gently until coated. Remove to large serving bowl.

Sprinkle with Parmesan cheese. Serves 6.

1 serving: *421 Calories; 9.4 g Total Fat (2.8 g Mono, 2 g Poly, 2.9 g Sat); 99 mg Cholesterol; 45 g Carbohydrate; 3 g Fibre; 31 g Protein; 328 mg Sodium*

Pictured on front cover.

Make Ahead: The night before, combine first 7 ingredients in slow cooker liner. Cover. Chill overnight. Add chicken. Cook as directed.

The Best Chicken Dish

Colourful and full of flavour, this is sure to become a favourite! Chickpeas and sweet red pepper accent this well-seasoned sauce. Delicious served over rice or pasta.

Cooking oil	**1 tbsp.**	**15 mL**
Lean ground chicken	**1 lb.**	**454 g**
Can of chickpeas (garbanzo beans), rinsed and drained	**19 oz.**	**540 mL**
Finely chopped onion	**1 cup**	**250 mL**
Salt	**1/4 tsp.**	**1 mL**
Sun-dried tomato pesto	**1/3 cup**	**75 mL**
All-purpose flour	**1 tbsp.**	**15 mL**
Can of diced tomatoes (with juice)	**14 oz.**	**398 mL**
Balsamic vinegar	**1 tbsp.**	**15 mL**
Granulated sugar	**1/2 tsp.**	**2 mL**
Salt	**1/4 tsp.**	**1 mL**
Chopped red pepper	**4 cups**	**1 L**
Finely chopped zucchini (with peel)	**1 cup**	**250 mL**

Heat cooking oil in large frying pan on medium. Add ground chicken. Scramble-fry for 5 to 10 minutes until no longer pink. Drain. Transfer to 3 1/2 to 4 quart (3.5 to 4 L) slow cooker.

Add chickpeas, onion and first amount of salt. Stir.

Stir pesto into flour in small bowl until smooth. Add next 4 ingredients. Stir well. Pour over chicken mixture. Stir well. Cover. Cook on Low for 8 to 10 hours or on High for 4 to 5 hours.

Add red pepper and zucchini. Stir. Cover. Cook on High for 30 to 45 minutes until red pepper is tender-crisp. Serves 8.

1 serving: *232 Calories; 11.2 g Total Fat (1.6 g Mono, 1.1 g Poly, 0.4 g Sat); 0 mg Cholesterol; 20 g Carbohydrate; 4 g Fibre; 14 g Protein; 353 mg Sodium*

Pictured on page 54.

Make Ahead: The night before, chop vegetables. Chill overnight in separate covered bowls. Scramble-fry ground chicken until no longer pink. Drain. Chill overnight in separate covered bowl. Assemble and cook as directed.

Chicken And Rice

Tender chicken and golden rice, speckled with tomato and peas. Cook on High for best results.

Cooking oil	1 tbsp.	15 mL
Bone-in, skinless chicken thighs	4	4
Chicken drumsticks, skin removed	4	4
Chopped onion	1 cup	250 mL
Garlic cloves, minced (or 1/2 tsp., 2 mL, powder)	2	2
Turmeric	1 tsp.	5 mL
Chili paste (sambal oelek)	1 tsp.	5 mL
Can of diced tomatoes (with juice)	28 oz.	796 mL
Converted white (or brown) rice	1 1/2 cups	375 mL
Prepared chicken broth	1 1/2 cups	375 mL
Chopped red pepper	1 cup	250 mL
Chopped celery	1/2 cup	125 mL
Salt	1/2 tsp.	2 mL
Pepper	1/4 tsp.	1 mL
Frozen peas	2/3 cup	150 mL

Heat cooking oil in large frying pan on medium. Add chicken thighs and drumsticks. Cook for 8 to 10 minutes, turning occasionally, until browned. Transfer to 3 1/2 to 4 quart (3.5 to 4 L) slow cooker.

Add onion to same large frying pan. Cook for 5 to 10 minutes, stirring often, until softened.

Add garlic, turmeric and chili paste. Heat and stir for about 1 minute until fragrant. Add to chicken. Stir.

Add next 7 ingredients. Stir well. Cover. Cook on High for 3 1/2 to 4 hours.

Add peas. Stir gently. Cover. Cook on High for 5 to 10 minutes until peas are heated through. Serves 4.

***1 serving:** 572 Calories; 11.9 g Total Fat (4.6 g Mono, 3.2 g Poly, 2.3 g Sat); 98 mg Cholesterol; 80 g Carbohydrate; 4 g Fibre; 35 g Protein; 982 mg Sodium*

Pictured on page 54.

Country Chicken Stew

A "thyme-ly" meal, ready when you are!
Serve this delicately seasoned, hearty stew in bread bowls.

Chopped onion	**1 cup**	**250 mL**
Chopped potato (with skin)	**2 cups**	**500 mL**
Sliced carrot	**2 cups**	**500 mL**
Shredded green cabbage, lightly packed	**2 cups**	**500 mL**
Chopped celery	**1/2 cup**	**125 mL**
Boneless, skinless chicken thighs	**3 1/2 lbs.**	**1.6 kg**
Prepared chicken broth	**2 cups**	**500 mL**
Can of condensed cream of mushroom soup	**10 oz.**	**284 mL**
Dried thyme	**1 tsp.**	**5 mL**
Salt	**1 1/2 tsp.**	**7 mL**
Pepper	**1 1/2 tsp.**	**7 mL**
Bay leaves	**2**	**2**
Prepared chicken broth	**1/4 cup**	**60 mL**
Cornstarch	**1/4 cup**	**60 mL**
Frozen peas	**1 cup**	**250 mL**

Layer first 6 ingredients, in order given, in 5 to 7 quart (5 to 7 L) slow cooker.

Combine next 5 ingredients in medium bowl. Pour over chicken. Add bay leaves. Do not stir. Cover. Cook on Low for 9 to 10 hours or on High for 4 1/2 to 5 hours. Remove and discard bay leaves.

Stir second amount of broth into cornstarch in small cup until smooth. Add to chicken mixture. Stir. Add peas. Stir well. Cover. Cook on High for 15 to 20 minutes until peas are heated through and sauce is thickened. Serves 14.

1 serving: *231 Calories; 8.2 g Total Fat (2.3 g Mono, 2.4 g Poly, 2.1 g Sat); 94 mg Cholesterol; 14 g Carbohydrate; 2 g Fibre; 25 g Protein; 596 mg Sodium*

Pictured on page 36.

Make Ahead: The night before, prepare vegetables (except potato) and prepare broth mixture. Chill overnight in separate covered bowls. Assemble and cook as directed.

Hearty Chicken Soup

Chunky vegetables, chicken and chickpeas fill this soup. A tasty combination to serve with buns or salad.

Prepared chicken broth	**6 cups**	**1.5 L**
Can of chickpeas (garbanzo beans), rinsed and drained	**14 oz.**	**398 mL**
Chopped onion	**1 1/2 cups**	**375 mL**
Chopped carrot	**1/2 cup**	**125 mL**
Chopped celery	**1/2 cup**	**125 mL**
Roma (plum) tomatoes, seeds removed, chopped	**3**	**3**
Tomato paste (see Tip, page 13)	**1/4 cup**	**60 mL**
Bay leaf	**1**	**1**
Pepper	**1/2 tsp.**	**2 mL**
Cooking oil	**2 tsp.**	**10 mL**
Boneless, skinless chicken thighs, chopped	**1 lb.**	**454 g**
Chopped fresh parsley (or 1 1/2 tsp., 7 mL, flakes), optional	**2 tbsp.**	**30 mL**

Combine first 9 ingredients in 3 1/2 to 4 quart (3.5 to 4 L) slow cooker.

Heat cooking oil in large frying pan on medium. Add chicken. Cook for about 5 minutes, stirring occasionally, until browned. Add to vegetable mixture. Stir. Cover. Cook on Low for 8 to 10 hours or on High for 4 to 5 hours. Remove and discard bay leaf.

Add parsley. Stir well. Makes about 11 cups (2.75 L).

1 cup (250 mL): *145 Calories; 4.8 g Total Fat (1.7 g Mono, 1.3 g Poly, 1 g Sat); 37 mg Cholesterol; 12 g Carbohydrate; 2 g Fibre; 14 g Protein; 511 mg Sodium*

Pictured on page 90.

Make Ahead: The night before, chop chicken thighs. Chill overnight in covered bowl. Prepare vegetables. Chill overnight in separate covered bowls. Assemble and cook as directed.

Chicken Chickpea Stew

Robust and filling. A fragrant stew loaded with chicken, chickpeas, pepperoni and tender vegetables.

Boneless, skinless chicken breast halves (4 – 6 oz., 113 – 170 g, each), each cut into 2 pieces	12	12
Can of chickpeas (garbanzo beans), rinsed and drained	19 oz.	540 mL
Sliced carrot	1 2/3 cups	400 mL
Chopped onion	1 cup	250 mL
Chopped green pepper	1 cup	250 mL
Deli pepperoni sticks, cut into 1/2 inch (12 mm) pieces	4 oz.	113 g
Can of tomato paste	5 1/2 oz.	156 mL
Water	2/3 cup	150 mL
Medium sherry	1/4 cup	60 mL
Salt	1/2 tsp.	2 mL
Chopped fresh basil (or 3/4 tsp., 4 mL, dried), see Note	1 tbsp.	15 mL
Chopped fresh thyme leaves (or 1/4 tsp., 1 mL, dried), see Note	1 tsp.	5 mL
Chopped fresh parsley (or 1/4 tsp., 1 mL, flakes), see Note	1 tsp.	5 mL

Layer first 6 ingredients, in order given, in 4 to 5 quart (4 to 5 L) slow cooker.

Combine next 4 ingredients in small bowl. Pour over pepperoni. Do not stir. Cover. Cook on Low for 8 to 9 hours or on High for 4 to 4 1/2 hours.

Add remaining 3 ingredients. Stir well. Cover. Cook on High for about 5 minutes until herbs are fragrant. Serves 6.

1 serving: *311 Calories; 7.3 g Total Fat (2.6 g Mono, 1.5 g Poly, 2.1 g Sat); 66 mg Cholesterol; 26 g Carbohydrate; 5 g Fibre; 34 g Protein; 541 mg Sodium*

Note: If using dried herbs, add to tomato paste mixture.

Make Ahead: The night before, prepare vegetables and prepare tomato paste mixture. Chill overnight in separate covered bowls. Assemble and cook as directed.

Lemon Chicken

Quick and easy to prepare in the morning.
Present this zesty, aromatic chicken on a large platter,
surrounded with colourful rice pilaf.

Whole chicken, rinsed and patted dry	**3 – 3 1/2 lbs.**	**1.4 – 1.6 kg**
Garlic cloves, coarsely chopped	**4**	**4**
Medium lemon, halved	**1**	**1**
Sprig of fresh rosemary	**1**	**1**
Dry white (or alcohol-free) wine	**1/2 cup**	**125 mL**
Sprigs of fresh rosemary	**2**	**2**
Worcestershire sauce	**2 tsp.**	**10 mL**
Salt	**1/4 tsp.**	**1 mL**
Pepper	**1/8 tsp.**	**0.5 mL**
Water	**2 tbsp.**	**30 mL**
Chicken gravy thickener (such as Bisto)	**2 tbsp.**	**30 mL**

Carefully loosen, but do not remove, skin around breast, thighs and legs of chicken. Stuff garlic evenly between meat and skin.

Place both lemon halves and first rosemary sprig inside chicken. Tie legs together with butcher's string. Tie wings to body.

Measure wine into 4 to 5 quart (4 to 5 L) slow cooker. Add chicken, breast-side up. Place remaining 2 rosemary sprigs beside chicken, 1 on each side.

Brush Worcestershire sauce evenly over chicken. Sprinkle with salt and pepper. Cover. Cook on Low for 8 to 10 hours or on High for 4 to 5 hours. Carefully remove chicken to large serving platter. Cover with foil. Let stand for 10 minutes. Skim and discard any fat from surface of liquid in slow cooker. Strain liquid through sieve into small saucepan. Discard solids.

Stir water into gravy thickener in small cup until smooth. Slowly add to liquid in saucepan, stirring constantly. Heat and stir on medium for about 5 minutes until boiling and thickened. Makes about 1 cup (250 mL) sauce. Remove and discard foil and butcher's string from chicken. Serve with sauce. Serves 4.

***1 serving:** 403 Calories; 20.8 g Total Fat (8.2 g Mono, 4.5 g Poly, 5.8 g Sat); 132 mg Cholesterol; 5 g Carbohydrate; trace Fibre; 42 g Protein; 561 mg Sodium*

Chicken Cacciatore

Easy to prepare and always a favourite! Serve over spaghetti and add crusty rolls on the side.

Chopped onion	1 1/2 cups	375 mL
Chopped celery	1 1/2 cups	375 mL
Chopped green pepper	1 1/2 cups	375 mL
Boneless, skinless chicken breast halves (4 – 6 oz., 113 – 170 g, each), each cut into 2 pieces	4	4
Boneless, skinless chicken thighs (2 – 3 oz., 57 – 85 g, each)	8	8
Can of crushed tomatoes	14 oz.	398 mL
Can of stewed tomatoes (with juice), chopped	14 oz.	398 mL
Garlic cloves, minced (or 1/2 tsp., 2 mL, powder)	2	2
Bay leaf	1	1
Dried whole oregano	1 1/2 tsp.	7 mL
Dried basil	1 tsp.	5 mL
Granulated sugar	1/2 tsp.	2 mL
Dried rosemary, crushed	1/2 tsp.	2 mL
Salt	1/2 tsp.	2 mL
Pepper	1/4 tsp.	1 mL

Layer first 5 ingredients, in order given, in 4 to 5 quart (4 to 5 L) slow cooker.

Combine remaining 10 ingredients in medium bowl. Pour over chicken. Do not stir. Cover. Cook on Low for 8 to 10 hours or on High for 4 to 5 hours. Remove and discard bay leaf. Serves 8.

1 serving: *210 Calories; 4.9 g Total Fat (1.4 g Mono, 1.3 g Poly, 1.2 g Sat); 92 mg Cholesterol; 12 g Carbohydrate; 2 g Fibre; 30 g Protein; 389 mg Sodium*

Make Ahead: The night before, chop vegetables and prepare tomato mixture. Chill overnight in separate covered bowls. Assemble and cook as directed.

Parmesan Chicken

When you just want something deliciously messy for dinner, serve this with fries and don't forget the napkins!

Plain yogurt	**3/4 cup**	**175 mL**
Chicken drumettes (or whole chicken wings, split in half and tips discarded)	**3 lbs.**	**1.4 kg**
Grated Parmesan cheese	**1 1/2 cups**	**375 mL**
Fine dry bread crumbs	**1/3 cup**	**75 mL**
Parsley flakes	**1 1/2 tsp.**	**7 mL**
Paprika	**1 1/2 tsp.**	**7 mL**
Seasoned salt	**1 1/2 tsp.**	**7 mL**

Measure yogurt into extra-large bowl. Add chicken. Stir until coated.

Combine remaining 5 ingredients in large resealable freezer bag. Add 1/3 of chicken. Seal bag. Toss until coated. Repeat twice with remaining 2/3 of chicken. Put chicken into greased 3 1/2 to 4 quart (3.5 to 4 L) slow cooker. Cover. Cook on Low for 8 to 9 hours or on High for 4 to 4 1/2 hours. Remove chicken with slotted spoon to large serving platter. Discard liquid. Serves 4.

1 serving: *389 Calories; 17.2 g Total Fat (4.8 g Mono, 1.4 g Poly, 9.2 g Sat); 96 mg Cholesterol; 12 g Carbohydrate; 1 g Fibre; 44 g Protein; 1387 mg Sodium*

Pictured on page 53.

1. Chicken Ratatouille, page 61
2. Parmesan Chicken, above

Props Courtesy Of: Emile Henry
Treasure Barrel

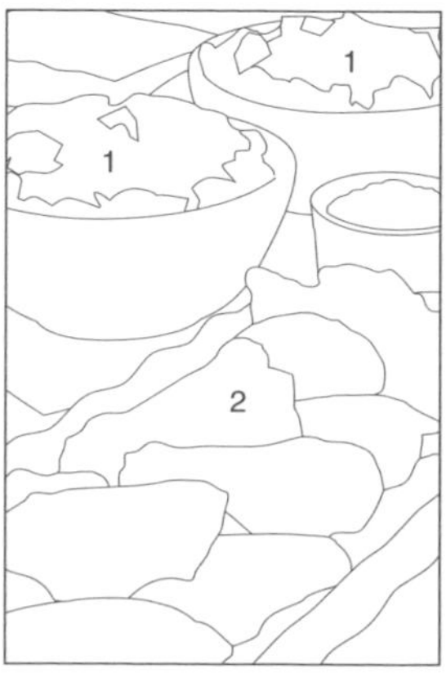

Barbecued Pulled Turkey

A tasty filling for soft tortillas, or a savoury topping for open-face buns. Serve with creamy coleslaw or potato salad.

Chopped onion	**1 cup**	**250 mL**
Boneless, skinless turkey thighs	**4 lbs.**	**1.8 kg**
Fancy (mild) molasses	**1/3 cup**	**75 mL**
Ketchup	**1/3 cup**	**75 mL**
White vinegar	**3 tbsp.**	**50 mL**
Worcestershire sauce	**2 tbsp.**	**30 mL**
Hot pepper sauce	**2 tsp.**	**10 mL**
Garlic salt	**1 tsp.**	**5 mL**
Liquid smoke (optional)	**1/2 tsp.**	**2 mL**
Pepper	**1/4 tsp.**	**1 mL**

Grease bottom and side of 4 to 5 quart (4 to 5 L) slow cooker liner with cooking spray. Spread onion evenly in bottom. Arrange turkey thighs over top.

Combine remaining 8 ingredients in small bowl. Pour over turkey. Do not stir. Cover. Cook on Low for 9 to 10 hours or on High for 4 1/2 to 5 hours. Transfer turkey with slotted spoon to large plate. Shred turkey with 2 forks. Return turkey to sauce. Stir well. Serves 12.

***1 serving:** 201 Calories; 5.1 g Total Fat (0 g Mono, 0 g Poly, 0 g Sat); 0 mg Cholesterol; 12 g Carbohydrate; trace Fibre; 27 g Protein; 222 mg Sodium*

Make Ahead: The night before, prepare molasses mixture. Chill overnight in covered bowl. Assemble and cook as directed.

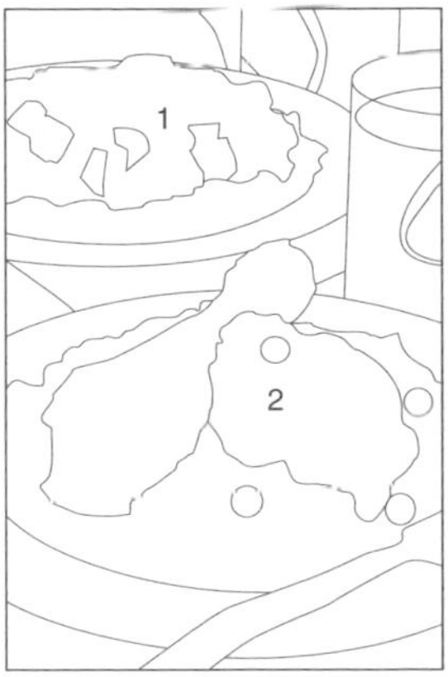

1. The Best Chicken Dish, page 45
2. Chicken And Rice, page 46

Props Courtesy Of: Cherison Enterprises Inc.
Danesco Inc.
Emile Henry
Pfaltzgraff Canada

Mild Turkey Chili

Colourful, with a light flavour. Serve with tortilla chips or crusty bread.

Cooking oil	2 tsp.	10 mL
Chopped onion	1 cup	250 mL
Chopped red pepper	1 cup	250 mL
Chili powder	1 tsp.	5 mL
Paprika	1 tsp.	5 mL
Ground cumin	1 tsp.	5 mL
Salt	1/4 tsp.	1 mL
Lean ground turkey	1 1/2 lbs.	680 g
Cans of red kidney beans (14 oz., 398 mL, each), rinsed and drained	2	2
Can of diced tomatoes (with juice)	14 oz.	398 mL
Tomato paste (see Tip, page 13)	2 tbsp.	30 mL
Diced jalapeño pepper, seeds and ribs removed (see Tip, page 95)	1 tbsp.	15 mL
Chopped fresh cilantro or parsley (or 1 1/2 tsp., 7 mL, dried)	2 tbsp.	30 mL

Heat cooking oil in large frying pan on medium. Add onion and red pepper. Cook for 5 to 10 minutes, stirring often, until onion is softened.

Add next 4 ingredients. Heat and stir for about 1 minute until fragrant.

Add ground turkey. Scramble-fry on medium-high for 5 to 10 minutes until turkey is no longer pink. Drain. Transfer to 3 1/2 to 4 quart (3.5 to 4 L) slow cooker.

Add next 4 ingredients. Stir well. Cover. Cook on Low for 10 to 11 hours or on High for 5 to 5 1/2 hours.

Add cilantro. Stir well. Serves 6.

1 serving: *318 Calories; 11.8 g Total Fat (4.5 g Mono, 3.1 g Poly, 2.8 g Sat); 90 mg Cholesterol; 26 g Carbohydrate; 7 g Fibre; 28 g Protein; 504 mg Sodium*

Pictured on page 144.

Make Ahead: The night before, chop vegetables and prepare kidney bean mixture. Chill overnight in separate covered bowls. Scramble-fry ground turkey until no longer pink. Drain. Chill overnight in separate covered bowl. Assemble and cook as directed.

Fragrant Spiced Chicken

A colourful, attractive dish with a Middle Eastern flair.
Serve with couscous and pita bread.

Cooking oil	1 tbsp.	15 mL
Boneless, skinless chicken thighs (2 – 3 oz., 57 – 85 g, each)	8	8
Chopped onion	1 1/2 cups	375 mL
Garlic cloves, minced (or 1 tsp., 5 mL, powder)	4	4
Ground cinnamon	1/2 tsp.	2 mL
Ground cumin	1/2 tsp.	2 mL
Can of chickpeas (garbanzo beans), rinsed and drained	19 oz.	540 mL
Can of diced tomatoes (with juice)	28 oz.	796 mL
Dried whole oregano	1 tsp.	5 mL
Salt	1/4 tsp.	1 mL
Fresh spinach, stems removed, lightly packed	2 cups	500 mL
Instant potato flakes	2 tbsp.	30 mL
Grated lemon zest	1/2 tsp.	2 mL

Heat cooking oil in large frying pan on medium. Add chicken. Cook for 8 to 10 minutes, turning occasionally, until browned. Transfer to large plate. Cover to keep warm.

Add next 4 ingredients to same large frying pan. Heat and stir for about 1 minute until fragrant. Spread evenly in bottom of 4 to 5 quart (4 to 5 L) slow cooker. Arrange chicken over top.

Combine next 4 ingredients in large bowl. Pour over chicken. Do not stir. Cover. Cook on Low for 8 to 9 hours or on High for 4 to 4 1/2 hours.

Add spinach, potato flakes and lemon zest. Stir gently. Cover. Heat on High for 1 to 2 minutes until spinach is wilted. Serves 4.

***1 serving:** 379 Calories; 12 g Total Fat (4.4 g Mono, 3.4 g Poly, 2.2 g Sat); 103 mg Cholesterol; 38 g Carbohydrate; 7 g Fibre; 32 g Protein; 764 mg Sodium*

Make Ahead: The night before, chop onion and prepare chickpea mixture. Chill overnight in separate covered bowls. Assemble and cook as directed.

Spicy Peanut Chicken

A spicy blend of interesting flavours makes this a great way to turn up the dial on dinner!

Cooking oil	1 tbsp.	15 mL
Bone-in, skinless chicken thighs	4	4
Chicken drumsticks, skin removed	4	4
Thinly sliced onion	1 1/2 cups	375 mL
Garlic cloves, minced (or 1/2 tsp., 2 mL, powder)	2	2
Curry powder	2 tsp.	10 mL
Dried crushed chilies	1 tsp.	5 mL
Prepared chicken broth	1/2 cup	125 mL
Tomato paste (see Tip, page 13)	1/4 cup	60 mL
Salt	1/4 tsp.	1 mL
Warm water	2 tbsp.	30 mL
Smooth peanut butter	1/3 cup	75 mL
Chopped red pepper	3/4 cup	175 mL
Chopped, peeled English cucumber	1/4 cup	60 mL
Coarsely chopped unsalted peanuts	2 tbsp.	30 mL
Chopped fresh cilantro or parsley (or 3/4 tsp., 4 mL, dried), optional	1 tbsp.	15 mL

Heat cooking oil in large frying pan on medium. Add chicken thighs and drumsticks. Cook for 8 to 10 minutes, turning occasionally, until browned. Transfer to 3 1/2 to 4 quart (3.5 to 4 L) slow cooker.

Add onion to same large frying pan. Cook for 5 to 10 minutes, stirring often, until softened.

Add next 3 ingredients. Heat and stir for about 1 minute until fragrant.

Add broth, tomato paste and salt. Stir well. Pour over chicken. Do not stir. Cover. Cook on Low for 8 to 9 hours or on High for 4 to 4 1/2 hours.

Stir warm water into peanut butter in small cup until smooth. Add to chicken mixture. Stir. Add red pepper. Stir well. Cover. Cook on High for about 15 minutes until red pepper is tender-crisp. Remove to large serving bowl.

(continued on next page)

Scatter cucumber, peanuts and cilantro over top. Serves 4.

1 serving: 408 Calories; 24.3 g Total Fat (10.6 g Mono, 6.6 g Poly, 4.7 g Sat); 98 mg Cholesterol; 18 g Carbohydrate; 4 g Fibre; 33 g Protein; 378 mg Sodium

Make Ahead: The night before, chop vegetables and prepare broth mixture. Chill overnight in separate covered bowls. Assemble and cook as directed.

Rich Chicken Ragoût

Rich and satisfying, this savoury stew (pronounced ra-GOO) is perfect served over egg noodles or rice. Port wine adds a unique accent to this filling dish.

All-purpose flour	**1/4 cup**	**60 mL**
Boneless, skinless chicken thighs (2 – 3 oz., 57 – 85 g, each)	**16**	**16**
Sliced fresh white mushrooms	**2 cups**	**500 mL**
Can of diced tomatoes (with juice)	**14 oz.**	**398 mL**
Thinly sliced red onion	**1 1/2 cups**	**375 mL**
Sun-dried tomatoes in oil, drained, chopped	**1/3 cup**	**75 mL**
Port wine	**3 – 4 tbsp.**	**50 – 60 mL**
Chopped fresh rosemary leaves (or 3/4 tsp., 4 mL, dried, crushed)	**1 tbsp.**	**15 mL**
Bay leaves	**2**	**2**
Salt	**1/4 tsp.**	**1 mL**
Pepper	**1/4 tsp.**	**1 mL**

Measure flour into large resealable freezer bag. Add 1/2 of chicken. Seal bag. Toss until coated. Repeat with remaining chicken. Transfer to 3 1/2 to 4 quart (3.5 to 4 L) slow cooker. Sprinkle with any remaining flour.

Combine remaining 9 ingredients in medium bowl. Pour over chicken. Cover. Cook on Low for 8 to 10 hours or on High for 4 to 5 hours. Remove and discard bay leaves. Serves 8.

1 serving: 203 Calories; 7.1 g Total Fat (2.3 g Mono, 1.7 g Poly, 1.7 g Sat); 93 mg Cholesterol; 10 g Carbohydrate; 1 g Fibre; 23 g Protein; 171 mg Sodium

Make Ahead: The night before, slice mushrooms and onion. Prepare tomato mixture. Chill overnight in covered bowl. Assemble and cook as directed.

Chicken Jambalaya

Chicken, sausage, shrimp and juicy vegetables—there's something for everyone in this spicy rice dish!

Boneless, skinless chicken thighs (2 – 3 oz., 57 – 85 g, each), halved	**8**	**8**
Cooking oil	**1 tsp.**	**5 mL**
Chorizo sausage, cut into 1/2 inch (12 mm) slices	**1 lb.**	**454 g**
Can of diced tomatoes (with juice)	**14 oz.**	**398 mL**
Chopped green pepper	**1 1/2 cups**	**375 mL**
Chopped onion	**1 cup**	**250 mL**
Chopped celery	**1 cup**	**250 mL**
Can of tomato sauce	**7 1/2 oz.**	**213 mL**
Garlic cloves, minced (or 1/2 tsp., 2 mL, powder)	**2**	**2**
Dried basil	**1/2 tsp.**	**2 mL**
Paprika	**1/2 tsp.**	**2 mL**
Dried crushed chilies	**1/4 – 1/2 tsp.**	**1 – 2 mL**
Dried thyme	**1/4 tsp.**	**1 mL**
Cooked long grain white rice (about 3/4 cup, 175 mL, uncooked)	**2 cups**	**500 mL**
Fresh uncooked medium shrimp, peeled and deveined	**1 lb.**	**454 g**

Put chicken into 3 1/2 to 4 quart (3.5 to 4 L) slow cooker.

Heat cooking oil in large frying pan on medium. Add sausage. Cook for about 5 minutes, stirring occasionally, until starting to brown. Remove to paper towels to drain.

Combine next 10 ingredients in large bowl. Pour over chicken. Add sausage. Stir well. Cover. Cook on Low for 8 to 9 hours or on High for 4 to 4 1/2 hours.

Add rice and shrimp. Stir gently. Cover. Cook on High for 15 to 20 minutes until shrimp are pink and curled. Serves 8.

1 serving: *507 Calories; 26.8 g Total Fat (12 g Mono, 3.5 g Poly, 9.3 g Sat); 183 mg Cholesterol; 26 g Carbohydrate; 2 g Fibre; 39 g Protein; 1051 mg Sodium*

(continued on next page)

Make Ahead: The night before, prepare tomato mixture. Chill overnight in covered bowl. Assemble and cook as directed.

Chicken Ratatouille

Pick up a crusty bread loaf on your way home to this aromatic, Italian-style stew (pronounced ra-tuh-TOO-ee). Serve over egg noodles.

Boneless, skinless chicken breast halves, cut into 1 inch (2.5 cm) pieces	**1 1/2 lbs.**	**680 g**
Eggplant, peeled, cut into 1 inch (2.5 cm) pieces	**1**	**1**
Cans of tomato sauce (14 oz., 398 mL, each)	**2**	**2**
Coarsely chopped zucchini (with peel)	**3 cups**	**750 mL**
Can of Italian-style stewed tomatoes	**14 oz.**	**398 mL**
Chopped green pepper	**1 cup**	**250 mL**
Chopped onion	**1 cup**	**250 mL**
Garlic cloves, minced (or 3/4 tsp., 4 mL, powder)	**3**	**3**
Granulated sugar	**1 tsp.**	**5 mL**
Dried basil	**1/2 tsp.**	**2 mL**
Dried whole oregano	**1/2 tsp.**	**2 mL**
Dried thyme	**1/2 tsp.**	**2 mL**
Pepper	**1/2 tsp.**	**2 mL**

Grated Parmesan cheese, for garnish

Combine first 13 ingredients in 5 to 7 quart (5 to 7 L) slow cooker. Cover. Cook on Low for 8 to 10 hours or on High for 4 to 5 hours. Remove to large serving bowl.

Sprinkle with Parmesan cheese. Serves 8.

1 serving: *179 Calories; 2 g Total Fat (0.4 g Mono, 0.5 g Poly, 0.5 g Sat); 49 mg Cholesterol; 20 g Carbohydrate; 5 g Fibre; 23 g Protein; 764 mg Sodium*

Pictured on page 53.

Make Ahead: The night before, cut up chicken. Chill overnight in covered bowl. Combine next 12 ingredients in slow cooker liner. Cover. Chill overnight. Add chicken to vegetable mixture the next morning. Stir well. Cook as directed.

Peppercorn Chicken

Green peppercorns add lively flavour to this saucy chicken and asparagus dish. Serve with rice.

All-purpose flour	2 tbsp.	30 mL
Boneless, skinless chicken thighs (2 – 3 oz., 57 – 85 g, each)	12	12
Cooking oil	1 tbsp.	15 mL
Cooking oil	2 tsp.	10 mL
Coarsely chopped celery	2 cups	500 mL
Large onion, cut into 8 wedges	1	1
Prepared chicken broth	1 1/2 cups	375 mL
Can of green peppercorns, drained	2 oz.	55 g
Dry onion soup mix, stir before measuring	2 tbsp.	30 mL
Prepared mustard	1 tbsp.	15 mL
Fresh asparagus, trimmed of tough ends, cut into 1 inch (2.5 cm) pieces	8 oz.	225 g
Sour cream	1/2 cup	125 mL

Measure flour into large resealable freezer bag. Add 1/2 of chicken. Seal bag. Toss until coated. Repeat with remaining chicken. Heat first amount of cooking oil in large frying pan on medium. Add chicken in 2 batches. Cook for 8 to 10 minutes per batch, turning occasionally, until browned. Transfer to 3 1/2 to 4 quart (3.5 to 4 L) slow cooker.

Heat second amount of cooking oil in same large frying pan on medium. Add celery and onion. Cook for 5 to 10 minutes, stirring often, until onion is softened. Add to chicken. Stir gently.

Combine next 4 ingredients in small bowl. Pour over chicken mixture. Do not stir. Cover. Cook on Low for 6 to 7 hours or on High for 3 to 3 1/2 hours.

Add asparagus and sour cream. Stir gently. Cover. Cook on High for about 10 minutes until asparagus is tender-crisp. Serves 6.

***1 serving:** 276 Calories; 13.9 g Total Fat (5.4 g Mono, 3.1 g Poly, 3.9 g Sat); 102 mg Cholesterol; 12 g Carbohydrate; 2 g Fibre; 26 g Protein; 735 mg Sodium*

Make Ahead: The night before, cut up vegetables and prepare broth mixture. Chill overnight in separate covered bowls. Assemble and cook as directed.

Beer And Bacon Chicken

Delightfully tender chicken in a smoky bacon and beer sauce.
Delicious served with buttered carrots and mashed potatoes.

All-purpose flour	**3 tbsp.**	**50 mL**
Chicken drumsticks, skin removed	**12**	**12**
Bacon slices, cooked crisp and crumbled	**4**	**4**
Can of beer	**12 1/2 oz.**	**355 mL**
Prepared chicken broth	**1/2 cup**	**125 mL**
Worcestershire sauce	**1 tbsp.**	**15 mL**
Chopped fresh oregano leaves (or 3/4 tsp., 4 mL, dried)	**1 tbsp.**	**15 mL**
Chopped fresh thyme leaves (or 1/2 tsp., 2 mL, dried)	**2 tsp.**	**10 mL**
Salt	**1/4 tsp.**	**1 mL**
Pepper	**1/4 tsp.**	**1 mL**
Water	**1 tbsp.**	**15 mL**
Cornstarch	**2 tsp.**	**10 mL**

Measure flour into large resealable freezer bag. Add 1/2 of chicken. Seal bag. Toss until coated. Repeat with remaining chicken. Put chicken into 3 1/2 to 4 quart (3.5 to 4 L) slow cooker.

Combine next 8 ingredients in 4 cup (1 L) liquid measure. Pour over chicken. Stir. Cover. Cook on Low for 8 to 9 hours or on High for 4 to 4 1/2 hours. Carefully remove chicken with slotted spoon to large serving bowl. Cover to keep warm.

Stir water into cornstarch in small cup until smooth. Add to liquid in slow cooker. Stir well. Cover. Cook on High for about 15 minutes until thickened. Pour over chicken. Serves 6.

__1 serving:__ 234 Calories; 8.9 g Total Fat (3.1 g Mono, 1.9 g Poly, 2.5 g Sat); 98 mg Cholesterol; 7 g Carbohydrate; trace Fibre; 26 g Protein; 268 mg Sodium

Make Ahead: The night before, remove and discard skin from chicken. Chill overnight in covered bowl. Prepare bacon mixture. Chill overnight in separate covered bowl. Assemble and cook as directed.

Paré Pointer

Even a spider wears a webbing dress to get married.

Oriental Chicken Legs

Simply delicious! Serve this tender chicken in ginger sauce with Oriental steam-fried noodles.

Bone-in chicken legs (backs attached), skin removed	**4**	**4**
Can of condensed chicken broth	**10 oz.**	**284 mL**
Rice vinegar	**1/4 cup**	**60 mL**
Low-sodium soy sauce	**1/4 cup**	**60 mL**
Brown sugar, packed	**2 tbsp.**	**30 mL**
Garlic cloves, minced (or 1/2 tsp., 2 mL, powder)	**2**	**2**
Piece of peeled gingerroot (1 inch, 2.5 cm), thinly sliced	**1**	**1**
Pepper	**1 tsp.**	**5 mL**
Water	**2 tbsp.**	**30 mL**
Cornstarch	**2 tbsp.**	**30 mL**
Chopped green onion	**2 tbsp.**	**30 mL**

Put chicken into 3 1/2 to 4 quart (3.5 to 4 L) slow cooker.

Combine next 7 ingredients in small bowl. Pour over chicken. Cover. Cook on Low for 8 to 9 hours or on High for 4 to 4 1/2 hours. Remove chicken with slotted spoon to large serving platter. Cover to keep warm. Skim and discard any fat from surface of liquid in slow cooker.

Stir water into cornstarch in small cup until smooth. Add to liquid in slow cooker. Stir. Add onion. Stir well. Cover. Cook on High for 15 to 20 minutes until sauce is slightly thickened. Makes about 1 1/2 cups (375 mL) sauce. Serve with chicken. Remove and discard ginger before serving, if desired. Serves 4.

1 serving: *302 Calories; 10.4 g Total Fat (3.9 g Mono, 2.4 g Poly, 2.9 g Sat); 120 mg Cholesterol; 14 g Carbohydrate; trace Fibre; 36 g Protein; 991 mg Sodium*

Make Ahead: The night before, remove and discard skin from chicken. Chill overnight in covered bowl. Prepare broth mixture. Chill overnight in separate covered bowl. Assemble and cook as directed.

Currant Thyme Pork

Stay "currant" with this thyme-ly recipe! The aroma of this dish will have everyone rushing to the kitchen to see what's cooking.

Chopped onion	**3/4 cup**	**175 mL**
Chopped carrot	**1 1/2 cups**	**375 mL**
Chopped parsnip	**1/2 cup**	**125 mL**
Red baby potatoes, larger ones cut in half	**2 lbs.**	**900 g**
All-purpose flour	**3 tbsp.**	**50 mL**
Boneless pork shoulder butt roast, trimmed of fat and cut into 3/4 inch (2 cm) pieces	**2 lbs.**	**900 g**
Cooking oil	**1 tbsp.**	**15 mL**
Sprigs of fresh thyme	**2**	**2**
Prepared chicken broth	**1 1/2 cups**	**375 mL**
Redcurrant jelly	**1/3 cup**	**75 mL**
Garlic cloves	**6**	**6**
Salt	**1/4 tsp.**	**1 mL**
Pepper	**1/2 tsp.**	**2 mL**
Chopped green onion	**1/4 cup**	**60 mL**

Layer first 4 ingredients, in order given, in 4 to 5 quart (4 to 5 L) slow cooker.

Measure flour into large resealable freezer bag. Add 1/2 of pork. Seal bag. Toss until coated. Repeat with remaining pork. Heat cooking oil in large frying pan on medium-high. Add pork in 2 batches. Cook for 8 to 10 minutes per batch, stirring occasionally, until browned. Scatter evenly on top of potatoes.

Place thyme sprigs on top of pork.

Combine next 5 ingredients in small bowl. Pour over pork. Do not stir. Cover. Cook on Low for 8 to 10 hours or on High for 4 to 5 hours. Remove and discard thyme sprigs.

Add green onion. Stir. Serves 8.

__1 serving:__ 351 Calories; 9.7 g Total Fat (4.5 g Mono, 1.5 g Poly, 2.8 g Sat); 71 mg Cholesterol; 37 g Carbohydrate; 4 g Fibre; 28 g Protein; 343 mg Sodium

Make Ahead: The night before, chop vegetables (except potatoes) and prepare broth mixture. Chill overnight in separate covered bowls. Assemble and cook as directed.

Pork And Mushroom Ragoût

Simple to prepare, with sophisticated flavour—white wine and tomato cream sauce coats tender pork and mushrooms. Serve over egg noodles.

All-purpose flour	**3 tbsp.**	**50 mL**
Boneless pork shoulder butt roast or steaks, trimmed of fat and cut into 3/4 inch (2 cm) pieces	**2 lbs.**	**900 g**
Cooking oil	**1 tbsp.**	**15 mL**
Cooking oil	**1 tbsp.**	**15 mL**
Sliced fresh white mushrooms	**2 1/2 cups**	**625 mL**
Large leek (white part only), thinly sliced	**1**	**1**
Prepared chicken broth	**1 1/4 cups**	**300 mL**
Dry white (or alcohol-free) wine	**1 cup**	**250 mL**
Tomato paste (see Tip, page 13)	**2 tbsp.**	**30 mL**
Salt	**1/4 tsp.**	**1 mL**
Pepper	**1/2 tsp.**	**2 mL**
Sour cream	**1/4 cup**	**60 mL**

Measure flour into large resealable freezer bag. Add 1/2 of pork. Seal bag. Toss until coated. Repeat with remaining pork. Heat first amount of cooking oil in large frying pan on medium-high. Add pork in 2 batches. Cook for 8 to 10 minutes per batch, stirring occasionally, until browned. Transfer to 3 1/2 to 4 quart (3.5 to 4 L) slow cooker.

Heat second amount of cooking oil in same large frying pan on medium. Add mushrooms and leek. Cook for about 5 minutes, stirring often, until leek is softened.

Slowly add broth, stirring constantly and scraping any brown bits from bottom of pan. Add next 4 ingredients. Heat and stir for about 2 minutes until boiling. Pour over pork. Do not stir. Cover. Cook on Low for 8 to 10 hours or on High for 4 to 5 hours.

Add sour cream. Stir well. Serves 8.

***1 serving:** 268 Calories; 12.4 g Total Fat (5.8 g Mono, 2 g Poly, 3.6 g Sat); 74 mg Cholesterol; 7 g Carbohydrate; 1 g Fibre; 26 g Protein; 293 mg Sodium*

Make Ahead: The night before, slice vegetables and prepare broth mixture. Chill overnight in separate covered bowls. Assemble and cook as directed.

Sweet Pork Sausage

Subtly sweet, with a mild curry flavour, this apple and raisin combination adds interest to tender pork sausage. Quick to assemble in the morning.

Small tart cooking apples (such as Granny Smith), peeled and cores removed, diced	**4**	**4**
Thinly sliced onion	**1 1/2 cups**	**375 mL**
Prepared chicken broth	**1 1/2 cups**	**375 mL**
Dark raisins	**1/3 cup**	**75 mL**
Curry paste	**1 tbsp.**	**15 mL**
Salt	**1/4 tsp.**	**1 mL**
Cooking oil	**1 tsp.**	**5 mL**
Thick pork sausages, cut into 1 inch (2.5 cm) pieces	**1 1/2 lbs.**	**680 g**
Water	**1 tbsp.**	**15 mL**
Cornstarch	**1 tbsp.**	**15 mL**
Pine nuts, toasted (see Tip, page 39), optional	**1 tbsp.**	**15 mL**
Chopped fresh parsley (or 1/2 tsp., 2 mL, flakes), optional	**2 tsp.**	**10 mL**

Combine first 6 ingredients in 3 1/2 to 4 quart (3.5 to 4 L) slow cooker.

Heat cooking oil in large frying pan on medium. Add sausage. Cook for 8 to 10 minutes, turning occasionally, until browned. Add to apple mixture. Stir well. Cover. Cook on Low for 8 to 10 hours or on High for 4 to 5 hours.

Stir water into cornstarch in small cup until smooth. Add to sausage mixture. Stir well. Cover. Cook on High for about 10 minutes until slightly thickened. Remove to large serving bowl.

Sprinkle with pine nuts and parsley. Serves 6.

__1 serving:__ 257 Calories; 12.5 g Total Fat (5.5 g Mono, 1.7 g Poly, 4 g Sat); 44 mg Cholesterol; 28 g Carbohydrate; 3 g Fibre; 10 g Protein; 719 mg Sodium

Paré Pointer

Everyone got tired of the pig telling so many jokes. He really was a boar!

Crock Of Herbed Pork

Fill your slow cooker with savoury pork seasoned with basil, oregano and a dash of sherry.

All-purpose flour	**2 tbsp.**	**30 mL**
Boneless pork shoulder butt roast or steaks, trimmed of fat and cut into 3/4 inch (2 cm) pieces	**1 1/2 lbs.**	**680 g**
Bacon slices, diced	**8**	**8**
Chopped carrot	**1 cup**	**250 mL**
Chopped onion	**1 cup**	**250 mL**
Prepared chicken broth	**1 cup**	**250 mL**
Dry sherry (or chicken broth)	**1/3 cup**	**75 mL**
Chopped fresh oregano leaves (or 3/4 tsp., 4 mL, dried)	**1 tbsp.**	**15 mL**
Salt	**1/4 tsp.**	**1 mL**
Pepper	**1/2 tsp.**	**2 mL**
Chopped fresh basil (see Note)	**2 tbsp.**	**30 mL**

Measure flour into large resealable freezer bag. Add pork. Seal bag. Toss until coated. Set aside.

Cook bacon in large frying pan on medium until crisp. Remove to paper towels to drain. Set aside. Remove and discard drippings, reserving 1 tbsp. (15 mL) in pan. Heat reserved drippings in same large frying pan on medium-high. Add pork. Cook for 8 to 10 minutes, stirring occasionally, until browned. Transfer to 3 1/2 to 4 quart (3.5 to 4 L) slow cooker.

Add bacon and next 7 ingredients. Stir well. Cover. Cook on Low for 8 to 10 hours or on High for 4 to 5 hours.

Add basil. Stir well. Serves 6.

1 serving: *289 Calories; 14.2 g Total Fat (6.5 g Mono, 1.7 g Poly, 5 g Sat); 81 mg Cholesterol; 8 g Carbohydrate; 1 g Fibre; 28 g Protein; 469 mg Sodium*

Note: Omit fresh basil. Add 1 1/2 tsp. (7 mL) dried basil to carrot mixture before cooking.

Make Ahead: The night before, trim and cut up pork. Chill overnight in covered bowl. Chop carrot and onion. Chill overnight in separate covered bowls. Assemble and cook as directed.

Pizza Topping Soup

Pizza you can eat with a spoon! Enjoy all the pizza toppings you love in a hearty soup. Serve with focaccia or crusty bread.

Cooking oil	**1 tsp.**	**5 mL**
Hot Italian sausages, casings removed, chopped	**1 lb.**	**454 g**
Cans of diced tomatoes (with juice), 14 oz. (398 mL) each	**2**	**2**
Sliced fresh white mushrooms	**2 cups**	**500 mL**
Sliced green pepper	**1 3/4 cups**	**425 mL**
Can of condensed beef broth	**10 oz.**	**284 mL**
Chopped onion	**1 cup**	**250 mL**
Water	**1 cup**	**250 mL**
Can of tomato sauce	**7 1/2 oz.**	**213 mL**
Dried whole oregano	**1/2 tsp.**	**2 mL**
Dried basil	**1/2 tsp.**	**2 mL**
Cayenne pepper	**1/8 tsp.**	**0.5 mL**
Grated part-skim mozzarella cheese	**1 cup**	**250 mL**

Heat cooking oil in medium frying pan on medium. Add sausage. Scramble-fry for 8 to 10 minutes until no longer pink. Drain. Transfer to 4 to 5 quart (4 to 5 L) slow cooker.

Add next 10 ingredients. Stir well. Cover. Cook on Low for 8 to 9 hours or on High for 4 to 4 1/2 hours. Makes about 9 1/3 cups (2.3 L) soup.

Divide and ladle soup into 6 individual bowls. Sprinkle each with cheese. Serves 6.

1 serving: *242 Calories; 13.3 g Total Fat (5.3 g Mono, 1.6 g Poly, 5.5 g Sat); 40 mg Cholesterol; 16 g Carbohydrate; 3 g Fibre; 16 g Protein; 1182 mg Sodium*

Make Ahead: The night before, prepare tomato mixture. Chill overnight in covered bowl. Assemble and cook as directed.

Paré Pointer

The shark's favourite game is swallow the leader.

Saucy Side Ribs

Succulent ribs in a sweet and sour sauce with a smoky barbecue accent.

Baby carrots	**1 lb.**	**454 g**
Pork side ribs, trimmed of fat and cut into 3-bone portions	**3 1/2 lbs.**	**1.6 kg**
Can of pineapple tidbits (with juice)	**14 oz.**	**398 mL**
Barbecue sauce	**1/3 cup**	**75 mL**
Apple cider vinegar	**3 tbsp.**	**50 mL**
Soy sauce	**3 tbsp.**	**50 mL**
Brown sugar, packed	**2 tbsp.**	**30 mL**
Garlic powder	**1 tsp.**	**5 mL**
Water	**3 tbsp.**	**50 mL**
Cornstarch	**3 tbsp.**	**50 mL**

Put carrots into 4 to 5 quart (4 to 5 L) slow cooker. Layer 1/2 of ribs on top of carrots.

Combine next 6 ingredients in medium bowl. Pour 1/2 of pineapple mixture over ribs. Layer remaining ribs on top. Pour remaining sauce over ribs. Do not stir. Cover. Cook on Low for 8 to 10 hours or on High for 4 to 5 hours. Remove ribs and carrots with slotted spoon to separate large serving bowls. Cover to keep warm. Skim and discard any fat from surface of liquid in slow cooker.

Stir water into cornstarch in small cup until smooth. Add to liquid in slow cooker. Stir well. Cover. Cook on High for about 10 minutes until thickened. Pour over ribs. Serve with carrots. Serves 8.

1 serving: *329 Calories; 12.7 g Total Fat (5.5 g Mono, 1.1 g Poly, 4.5 g Sat); 79 mg Cholesterol; 23 g Carbohydrate; 3 g Fibre; 31 g Protein; 533 mg Sodium*

Make Ahead: The night before, prepare pineapple mixture. Chill overnight in covered bowl. Assemble and cook as directed.

1. Mint And Cider Pork, page 92
2. Corny Shepherd's Pie, page 76

Props Courtesy Of: Cherison Enterprises Inc.
Pfaltzgraff Canada
The Bay
Totally Bamboo

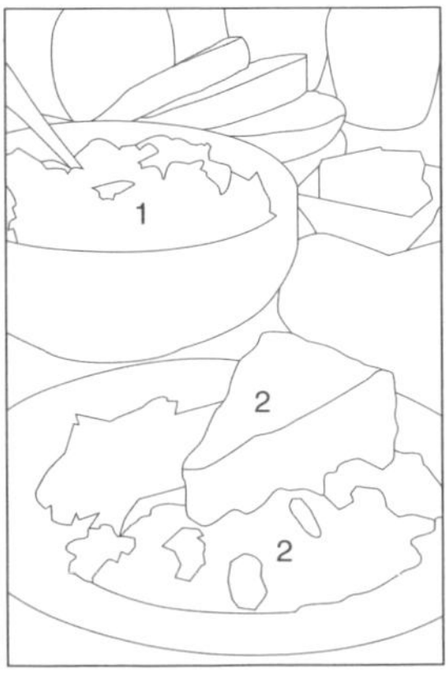

Savoury Side Ribs

Allspice and cinnamon make these saucy ribs a bit different from most.

Garlic powder	**1 tsp.**	**5 mL**
Ground ginger	**1 tsp.**	**5 mL**
Dry mustard	**1 tsp.**	**5 mL**
Onion powder	**1 tsp.**	**5 mL**
Cayenne pepper	**1/2 tsp.**	**2 mL**
Ground allspice	**1/4 tsp.**	**1 mL**
Ground cinnamon	**1/4 tsp.**	**1 mL**
Pork side ribs, trimmed of fat and cut into 3-bone portions	**3 1/2 lbs.**	**1.6 kg**
Large onion, thinly sliced	**1**	**1**
Barbecue sauce	**1 cup**	**250 mL**
Water	**1/2 cup**	**125 mL**
Chili sauce	**1/3 cup**	**75 mL**

Combine first 7 ingredients in small cup. Divide and sprinkle over both sides of each rib portion. Layer ribs alternately with onion slices in 4 to 5 quart (4 to 5 L) slow cooker.

Combine barbecue sauce, water and chili sauce in small bowl. Pour over ribs. Do not stir. Cover. Cook on Low for 8 to 10 hours or on High for 4 to 5 hours. Remove ribs with slotted spoon to large serving platter. Skim and discard any fat from surface of liquid in slow cooker. Makes about 2 cups (500 mL) sauce. Serve with ribs. Serves 8.

1 serving: *282 Calories; 12.8 g Total Fat (5.8 g Mono, 1.6 g Poly, 4.3 g Sat); 90 mg Cholesterol; 10 g Carbohydrate; 3 g Fibre; 31 g Protein; 521 mg Sodium*

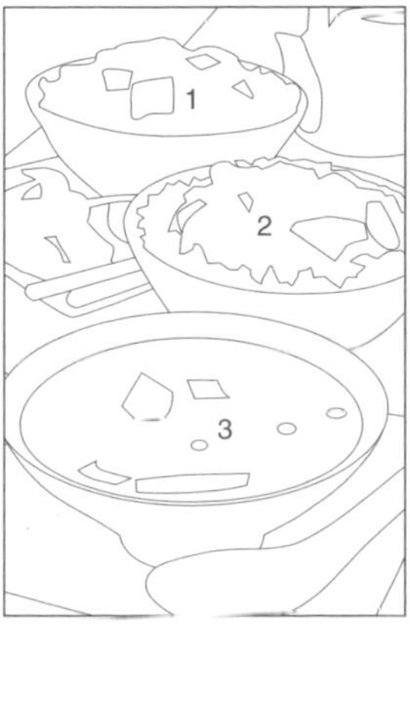

1. Sweet And Sour Pork, page 75
2. Snappy Pineapple Chicken, page 42
3. Chinese Mushroom Soup, page 77

Props Courtesy Of: Pier 1 Imports
Scona Clayworks

Fruity Pork Roast

Cooked on Low, this tender pork roast with a rich, sweet fruit sauce is sure to delight! Serve with roasted baby potatoes.

Bacon slices, diced	**4**	**4**
Boneless pork shoulder butt roast, trimmed of fat	**3 lbs.**	**1.4 kg**
Chopped onion	**1 cup**	**250 mL**
Garlic clove, minced (or 1/4 tsp., 1 mL, powder)	**1**	**1**
All-purpose flour	**1/4 cup**	**60 mL**
Orange juice	**1 1/2 cups**	**375 mL**
Medium bananas, mashed	**2**	**2**
Dried apricots, halved	**1/2 cup**	**125 mL**
Dried pitted prunes, halved	**1/2 cup**	**125 mL**
Bay leaf	**1**	**1**
Ground allspice	**1/4 tsp.**	**1 mL**
Ground cinnamon	**1/4 tsp.**	**1 mL**
Dried crushed chilies	**1/4 tsp.**	**1 mL**
Grated orange zest	**1/2 – 1 tsp.**	**2 – 5 mL**

Cook bacon in large frying pan on medium until crisp. Remove to paper towels to drain. Set aside. Remove and discard drippings, reserving 1 tbsp. (15 mL) in pan.

Heat reserved drippings in same large frying pan on medium. Add roast. Cook for about 10 minutes, turning occasionally, until browned on all sides. Transfer to 3 1/2 to 4 quart (3.5 to 4 L) slow cooker.

Add onion and garlic to same large frying pan. Cook for about 2 minutes, stirring often, until starting to brown.

Add flour. Heat and stir for 1 minute. Slowly add orange juice, stirring constantly, until boiling and thickened.

Add bacon and next 7 ingredients. Stir well. Pour over roast. Cover. Cook on Low for 8 to 10 hours. Remove roast to large serving platter. Cover to keep warm. Skim and discard any fat from surface of liquid in slow cooker. Remove and discard bay leaf.

(continued on next page)

Add orange zest to liquid in slow cooker. Stir well. Makes about 4 1/2 cups (1.1 L) sauce. Cut roast into thin slices. Serve with sauce. Makes 12 servings (2 to 3 oz., 57 to 85 g each, cooked weight).

__1 serving:__ 273 Calories; 9.9 g Total Fat (4.4 g Mono, 1.1 g Poly, 3.4 g Sat); 74 mg Cholesterol; 20 g Carbohydrate; 2 g Fibre; 26 g Protein; 116 mg Sodium

Make Ahead: The night before, cut up dried fruit and store in covered small bowl. Combine spices in small cup. Cover. Dice bacon and chop onion. Chill overnight in separate covered bowls. Assemble and cook as directed.

Sweet And Sour Pork

Tender pork in a sweet sauce accented with pineapple. Serve over noodles.

Chopped onion	**1 cup**	**250 mL**
Diced carrot	**1 cup**	**250 mL**
Apple cider vinegar	**1/4 cup**	**60 mL**
Brown sugar, packed	**1/4 cup**	**60 mL**
Soy sauce	**2 tbsp.**	**30 mL**
Ketchup	**2 tbsp.**	**30 mL**
Garlic cloves, minced (or 1/2 tsp., 2 mL, powder)	**2**	**2**
Ground ginger	**1 tsp.**	**5 mL**
Pork stew meat	**2 lbs.**	**900 g**
Water	**2 tbsp.**	**30 mL**
Cornstarch	**2 tbsp.**	**30 mL**
Can of pineapple tidbits (with juice)	**14 oz.**	**398 mL**
Chopped green pepper	**1 cup**	**250 mL**

Combine first 9 ingredients in 3 1/2 to 4 quart (3.5 to 4 L) slow cooker. Cover. Cook on Low for 8 to 9 hours or on High for 4 to 4 1/2 hours.

Stir water into cornstarch in small cup until smooth. Add to pork mixture. Stir. Add pineapple and green pepper. Stir well. Cover. Cook on High for about 15 minutes until green pepper is tender-crisp and sauce is thickened. Serves 8.

__1 serving:__ 365 Calories; 20.4 g Total Fat (9 g Mono, 2.2 g Poly, 7.1 g Sat); 80 mg Cholesterol; 25 g Carbohydrate; 2 g Fibre; 21 g Protein; 398 mg Sodium

Pictured on page 72 and on back cover.

Make Ahead: The night before, combine first 8 ingredients in slow cooker liner. Cover. Chill overnight. Add pork. Cook as directed.

Corny Shepherd's Pie

Tender polenta (poh-LEN-tah), a mixture of cornmeal and cheese, tops spicy sausage and tender vegetables in this "crock pot pie."

Cooking oil	**1 tsp.**	**5 mL**
Hot Italian sausages, casings removed, chopped	**1 lb.**	**454 g**
Lean ground pork	**1 lb.**	**454 g**
Chopped onion	**1/2 cup**	**125 mL**
Chopped celery	**1/2 cup**	**125 mL**
Cans of diced tomatoes (with juice), 14 oz. (398 mL) each	**2**	**2**
Frozen kernel corn	**1 cup**	**250 mL**
Dried whole oregano	**1 tsp.**	**5 mL**
CORNMEAL TOPPING		
Water	**3 cups**	**750 mL**
Hard margarine (or butter)	**1 tbsp.**	**15 mL**
Pepper	**1/4 tsp.**	**1 mL**
Yellow regular (or coarse) cornmeal	**1 cup**	**250 mL**
Grated Parmesan cheese	**1/2 cup**	**125 mL**
Parsley flakes	**2 tsp.**	**10 mL**

Heat cooking oil in large frying pan on medium. Add next 4 ingredients. Scramble-fry for 8 to 10 minutes until sausage and ground pork are no longer pink. Drain. Transfer to 3 1/2 to 4 quart (3.5 to 4 L) slow cooker.

Add tomatoes, corn and oregano. Stir well.

Cornmeal Topping: Measure water into medium saucepan. Bring to a boil on medium-high. Add margarine and pepper. Reduce heat to low. Slowly add cornmeal, stirring constantly, until water is absorbed. Cook for 2 to 3 minutes, stirring occasionally, until mixture is very thick.

Add Parmesan cheese and parsley. Stir well. Spread evenly on top of sausage mixture. Cover. Cook on Low for 8 to 9 hours or on High for 4 to 4 1/2 hours. Serves 8.

1 serving: *363 Calories; 19.8 g Total Fat (8.8 g Mono, 2.3 g Poly, 7.1 g Sat); 63 mg Cholesterol; 25 g Carbohydrate; 2 g Fibre; 22 g Protein; 588 mg Sodium*

(continued on next page)

Pictured on page 71.

Make Ahead: The night before, chop onion and celery. Chill overnight in separate covered bowls. Assemble and cook as directed.

Chinese Mushroom Soup

A mingling of light ingredients, reminiscent of hot and sour soup.

Chinese dried mushrooms, stems removed	**15**	**15**
Boiling water		
Prepared chicken broth	**6 cups**	**1.5 L**
Can of sliced water chestnuts, drained	**8 oz.**	**227 mL**
Can of bamboo shoots, drained	**8 oz.**	**227 mL**
Rice vinegar	**1/3 cup**	**75 mL**
Soy sauce	**1/4 cup**	**60 mL**
Dried crushed chilies	**1 tsp.**	**5 mL**
Diced cooked pork	**1 cup**	**250 mL**
Sliced green onion	**2 tbsp.**	**30 mL**

Place mushrooms in small bowl. Add boiling water until 2 inches (5 cm) above mushrooms. Let stand for about 20 minutes until softened. Drain. Thinly slice mushrooms. Transfer to 3 1/2 to 4 quart (3.5 to 4 L) slow cooker.

Add next 6 ingredients. Stir well. Cover. Cook on Low for 8 to 10 hours or on High for 4 to 5 hours.

Add pork and onion. Stir well. Cover. Cook on High for 10 to 15 minutes until pork is heated through. Makes about 8 1/2 cups (2.1 L).

1 cup (250 mL): *117 Calories; 3.9 g Total Fat (1.6 g Mono, 0.5 g Poly, 1.2 g Sat); 14 mg Cholesterol; 11 g Carbohydrate; 1 g Fibre; 10 g Protein; 1110 mg Sodium*

Pictured on page 72 and on back cover.

Variation: Omit pork. Use same amount of diced cooked beef, chicken or shrimp. For meatless soup, use same amount of diced tofu.

Make Ahead: The night before, combine prepared mushrooms and broth mixture in slow cooker liner. Cover. Chill overnight. Assemble and cook as directed.

Hot And Spicy Pork

Spice things up with this pottage of pork and yam. Excellent with rice or noodles.

Chopped onion	1 cup	250 mL
Chopped carrot	1 cup	250 mL
All-purpose flour	3 tbsp.	50 mL
Pork shoulder butt roast or steaks, trimmed of fat and cut into 3/4 inch (2 cm) pieces	2 lbs.	900 g
Cooking oil	1 tbsp.	15 mL
Ground cumin	1 tsp.	5 mL
Paprika	1 tsp.	5 mL
Ground turmeric	1 tsp.	5 mL
Prepared chicken broth	1 1/2 cups	375 mL
Chili paste (sambal oelek)	1 tbsp.	15 mL
Salt	1/4 tsp.	1 mL
Yams (or sweet potatoes), peeled, cut into 1/2 inch (12 mm) pieces	1 lb.	454 g
Chopped fresh cilantro or parsley (or 1 1/2 tsp., 7 mL, dried)	2 tbsp.	30 mL
Sour cream	2 tbsp.	30 mL

Put onion and carrot into 3 1/2 to 4 quart (3.5 to 4 L) slow cooker.

Measure flour into large resealable freezer bag. Add 1/2 of pork. Seal bag. Toss until coated. Repeat with remaining pork. Heat cooking oil in large frying pan on medium. Add pork in 2 batches. Cook for 5 to 10 minutes per batch, stirring occasionally, until browned. Arrange on top of vegetables.

Add cumin, paprika and turmeric to same large frying pan. Heat and stir on medium for about 1 minute until fragrant.

Slowly add broth, stirring constantly and scraping any brown bits from bottom of pan. Add chili paste and salt. Heat and stir for 1 to 2 minutes until hot. Pour over pork. Do not stir. Cover. Cook on Low for 8 to 10 hours or on High for 4 to 5 hours.

Add yam. Stir well. Cover. Cook on High for about 45 minutes until yam is tender.

(continued on next page)

Add cilantro and sour cream. Stir well. Serves 8.

1 serving: 299 Calories; 10.3 g Total Fat (4.7 g Mono, 1.5 g Poly, 3.1 g Sat); 72 mg Cholesterol; 24 g Carbohydrate; 4 g Fibre; 27 g Protein; 329 mg Sodium

Make Ahead: The night before, prepare vegetables (except yam). Chill overnight in separate covered bowls. Assemble and cook as directed.

Apricot Pork Roast

Gently sweet apricot and zesty citrus flavours blend nicely in a delicious sauce to complement tender pork roast.

Cooking oil	**1 tbsp.**	**15 mL**
Boneless pork shoulder butt roast, trimmed of fat	**3 lbs.**	**1.4 kg**
Chopped dried apricot	**1 cup**	**250 mL**
Dry white (or alcohol-free) wine	**1/2 cup**	**125 mL**
Orange juice	**1/2 cup**	**125 mL**
Dry onion soup mix, stir before measuring	**2 tbsp.**	**30 mL**
Pepper	**1/2 tsp.**	**2 mL**
Water	**2 tbsp.**	**30 mL**
Cornstarch	**1 1/2 tbsp.**	**25 mL**
Plain yogurt (or sour cream)	**2 tbsp.**	**30 mL**

Heat cooking oil in large frying pan on medium-high. Add roast. Cook for 5 to 10 minutes, turning occasionally, until browned on all sides. Transfer to 4 to 5 quart (4 to 5 L) slow cooker.

Combine next 5 ingredients in small bowl. Pour over roast. Cover. Cook on Low for 8 to 10 hours or on High for 4 to 5 hours. Remove roast to large serving platter. Cover to keep warm. Skim and discard any fat from surface of liquid in slow cooker.

Stir water into cornstarch in small cup until smooth. Add yogurt. Stir. Add to liquid in slow cooker. Stir well. Cover. Cook on High for 10 to 15 minutes until boiling and thickened. Makes about 1 1/4 cups (300 mL) sauce. Cut roast into thin slices. Serve with sauce. Makes 12 servings (2 to 3 oz., 57 to 85 g each, cooked weight).

1 serving: 233 Calories; 8.9 g Total Fat (4.2 g Mono, 1.2 g Poly, 2.7 g Sat); 72 mg Cholesterol; 11 g Carbohydrate; 1 g Fibre; 25 g Protein; 307 mg Sodium

Make Ahead: The night before, prepare apricot mixture. Chill overnight in covered bowl. Assemble and cook as directed.

Sweet Lamb Curry

A rich, Middle Eastern-flavoured dish. Serve over rice or couscous.

Cooking oil	**2 tbsp.**	**30 mL**
Lamb stew meat	**2 lbs.**	**900 g**
Thinly sliced onion	**2 cups**	**500 mL**
Cinnamon stick (4 inches, 10 cm)	**1**	**1**
Garlic cloves, minced (or 1 tsp., 5 mL, powder)	**4**	**4**
Whole green cardamom, bruised (see Tip, page 99)	**6**	**6**
Finely grated, peeled gingerroot (or 1/2 tsp., 2 mL, ground ginger)	**2 tsp.**	**10 mL**
Ground cumin	**1 tsp.**	**5 mL**
Ground coriander	**1 tsp.**	**5 mL**
Dried crushed chilies	**1 tsp.**	**5 mL**
Salt	**1/4 tsp.**	**1 mL**
Prepared chicken broth	**2/3 cup**	**150 mL**
Tart medium cooking apples (such as Granny Smith), peeled and cores removed, diced	**3**	**3**
Can of coconut milk	**14 oz.**	**398 mL**
Cornstarch	**4 tsp.**	**20 mL**
Dark raisins	**1/2 cup**	**125 mL**

Heat cooking oil in large frying pan on medium. Add lamb in 2 batches. Cook for 5 to 10 minutes per batch, stirring occasionally, until browned. Transfer with slotted spoon to 3 1/2 to 4 quart (3.5 to 4 L) slow cooker.

Add onion to same large frying pan. Cook for 5 to 10 minutes, stirring often, until softened. Add next 8 ingredients. Heat and stir for 1 to 2 minutes until fragrant.

Slowly add broth, stirring constantly and scraping any brown bits from bottom of pan. Pour over lamb.

Add apple. Stir well. Cover. Cook on Low for 8 to 9 hours or on High for 4 to 4 1/2 hours. Remove and discard cinnamon stick and cardamom.

Stir coconut milk into cornstarch in small bowl until smooth. Add to lamb mixture. Stir. Add raisins. Stir well. Cover. Cook on High for about 20 minutes until slightly thickened. Serves 8.

(continued on next page)

1 serving: 367 Calories; 20.1 g Total Fat (5 g Mono, 1.8 g Poly, 11.5 g Sat); 73 mg Cholesterol; 24 g Carbohydrate; 2 g Fibre; 25 g Protein; 155 mg Sodium

Make Ahead: The night before, combine spices in small cup. Cover. Slice onion. Chill overnight in covered bowl. Assemble and cook as directed.

Rosemary Lamb

Hearty lamb shanks in a rustic red wine and rosemary sauce. Serve with garlic mashed potatoes and spinach.

Coarsely chopped carrot	**2 cups**	**500 mL**
Thinly sliced onion	**1 cup**	**250 mL**
All-purpose flour	**1/4 cup**	**60 mL**
Salt	**1/2 tsp.**	**2 mL**
Pepper	**1/2 tsp.**	**2 mL**
Lamb shanks (2 1/2 – 3 lbs., 1.1 – 1.4 kg, each)	**4**	**4**
Cooking oil	**1 tbsp.**	**15 mL**
Dry red (or alcohol-free) wine	**2/3 cup**	**150 mL**
Tomato paste (see Tip, page 13)	**2 tbsp.**	**30 mL**
Chopped fresh rosemary leaves (or 1 1/4 tsp., 6 mL, dried, crushed)	**1 1/2 tbsp.**	**25 mL**

Put carrot and onion into 5 to 7 quart (5 to 7 L) slow cooker.

Combine next 3 ingredients in large resealable freezer bag. Add 1/2 of lamb shanks. Seal bag. Toss until coated. Repeat with remaining lamb. Heat cooking oil in large frying pan on medium-high. Add lamb in 2 batches, reserving any remaining flour mixture. Cook for 5 to 7 minutes per batch, turning occasionally, until browned. Arrange on top of vegetables. Sprinkle with remaining flour mixture.

Combine remaining 3 ingredients in 2 cup (500 mL) liquid measure. Pour over lamb. Cover. Cook on Low for 8 to 10 hours or on High for 4 to 5 hours. Remove lamb to large serving platter. Cover to keep warm. Skim and discard any fat from surface of liquid in slow cooker. Drizzle liquid from slow cooker over individual servings. Serves 4.

1 serving: 481 Calories; 25.7 g Total Fat (11 g Mono, 2.9 g Poly, 9.8 g Sat); 118 mg Cholesterol; 21 g Carbohydrate; 4 g Fibre; 34 g Protein; 478 mg Sodium

Make Ahead: The night before, prepare vegetables and prepare wine mixture. Chill overnight in separate covered bowls. Assemble and cook as directed.

Leg Of Lamb

A complete meal awaits! Tender lamb and herb-crusted vegetables cooked to perfection in a sensational pesto and wine sauce.

Medium onions, chopped	3	3
Garlic cloves, minced (or 3/4 tsp., 4 mL, powder)	3	3
Whole leg of lamb roast, trimmed of fat	3 3/4 – 4 lbs.	1.7 – 1.8 kg
Baby potatoes, larger ones cut in half	2 lbs.	900 g
Baby carrots	2 lbs.	900 g
Dry red (or alcohol-free) wine	1 1/2 cups	375 mL
Water	1 1/2 cups	375 mL
Jar of sun-dried tomato pesto	9 1/2 oz.	270 mL
Parsley flakes	1 tbsp.	15 mL
Dried rosemary, crushed	2 tsp.	10 mL
Dried whole oregano	2 tsp.	10 mL
Pepper	1 tsp.	5 mL
Water	2 tbsp.	30 mL
Cornstarch	4 tsp.	20 mL

Put onion and garlic into 7 quart (7 L) slow cooker. Place roast on top.

Arrange potatoes and carrots around roast.

Combine next 7 ingredients in large bowl. Pour over roast. Cover. Cook on Low for 8 to 10 hours or on High for 4 to 5 hours. Remove roast to large serving platter. Cover to keep warm. Remove vegetables with slotted spoon to large serving bowl. Cover to keep warm. Skim and discard any fat from surface of liquid in slow cooker.

Stir water into cornstarch in small cup until smooth. Add to liquid in slow cooker. Stir well. Cover. Cook on High for 15 to 20 minutes until slightly thickened. Makes about 4 cups (1 L) sauce. Cut roast into thin slices. Makes 10 servings of meat (2 to 3 oz., 57 to 85 g each, cooked weight). Serve with sauce and vegetables. Serves 10.

***1 serving:** 319 Calories; 7.1 g Total Fat (3.1 g Mono, 0.9 g Poly, 2.1 g Sat); 70 mg Cholesterol; 32 g Carbohydrate; 4 g Fibre; 27 g Protein; 143 mg Sodium*

Make Ahead: The night before, chop onions and prepare wine mixture. Chill overnight in separate covered bowls. Assemble and cook as directed.

Easy Lamb Ragoût

Juicy pieces of lamb and tender vegetables seasoned with fragrant herbs—a delicious meal that's quick and easy to prepare. Serve with a crisp salad.

Medium carrots, cut into 1/2 inch (12 mm) slices	**4**	**4**
Red baby potatoes, quartered	**1 lb.**	**454 g**
Fennel bulb (white part only), halved and thinly sliced	**1**	**1**
All-purpose flour	**1/4 cup**	**60 mL**
Lamb stew meat	**1 1/2 lbs.**	**680 g**
Prepared beef broth	**1 cup**	**250 mL**
Dry white (or alcohol-free) wine	**1/2 cup**	**125 mL**
Garlic clove, minced (or 1/4 tsp., 1 mL, powder)	**1**	**1**
Dill weed	**1/2 tsp.**	**2 mL**
Dried marjoram	**1/2 tsp.**	**2 mL**
Salt	**1/2 tsp.**	**2 mL**
Pepper	**1/4 tsp.**	**1 mL**

Layer first 3 ingredients, in order given, in 4 to 5 quart (4 to 5 L) slow cooker.

Measure flour into large resealable freezer bag. Add lamb. Seal bag. Toss until coated. Scatter lamb evenly over fennel. Sprinkle with any remaining flour.

Combine remaining 7 ingredients in small bowl. Pour over lamb. Do not stir. Cover. Cook on Low for 8 to 10 hours or on High for 4 to 5 hours. Serves 6.

1 serving: *282 Calories; 6.4 g Total Fat (2.5 g Mono, 0.7 g Poly, 2.2 g Sat); 74 mg Cholesterol; 26 g Carbohydrate; 3 g Fibre; 27 g Protein; 455 mg Sodium*

Make Ahead: The night before, cut up vegetables (except potatoes) and prepare broth mixture. Chill overnight in separate covered bowls. Assemble and cook as directed.

Paré Pointer

Mrs. Owl left Mr. Owl because he didn't give a hoot.

Lamb With Spinach

Vibrant green spinach and red, juicy tomatoes add wonderful colour to delicately seasoned lamb. Serve with couscous.

Cooking oil	1 tbsp.	15 mL
Lamb stew meat	2 lbs.	900 g
Sliced fresh white mushrooms	2 cups	500 mL
Chopped onion	1 cup	250 mL
Chopped red pepper	1 cup	250 mL
Can of diced tomatoes (with juice)	14 oz.	398 mL
Prepared chicken broth	1 cup	250 mL
Chopped fresh thyme leaves (or 1/2 tsp., 2 mL, dried)	2 tsp.	10 mL
Granulated sugar	1/2 tsp.	2 mL
Salt	1/4 tsp.	1 mL
Pepper	1/4 tsp.	1 mL
Water	1 tbsp.	15 mL
Cornstarch	1 tbsp.	15 mL
Fresh spinach, stems removed, lightly packed	2 cups	500 mL
Chopped fresh basil (see Note)	2 tbsp.	30 mL

Heat cooking oil in large frying pan on medium-high. Add lamb in 2 batches. Cook for 8 to 10 minutes per batch, stirring occasionally, until browned. Transfer to 3 1/2 to 4 quart (3.5 to 4 L) slow cooker.

Add mushrooms, onion and red pepper to same large frying pan. Cook on medium for 5 to 10 minutes, stirring often, until onion is softened. Add to lamb. Stir.

Combine next 6 ingredients in medium bowl. Pour over lamb mixture. Stir well. Cover. Cook on Low for 8 to 10 hours or on High for 4 to 5 hours.

Stir water into cornstarch in small cup until smooth. Add to lamb mixture. Stir well. Cover. Cook on High for 5 to 10 minutes until sauce is thickened.

Add spinach and basil. Stir well. Serves 8.

(continued on next page)

1 serving: 208 Calories; 8.2 g Total Fat (3.5 g Mono, 1.2 g Poly, 2.4 g Sat); 73 mg Cholesterol; 8 g Carbohydrate; 2 g Fibre; 25 g Protein; 346 mg Sodium

Pictured on page 89.

Note: Omit fresh basil. Add 1 1/2 tsp. (7 mL) dried basil to tomato mixture before cooking.

Make Ahead: The night before, prepare vegetables and prepare tomato mixture. Chill overnight in separate covered bowls. Assemble and cook as directed.

Sun-Dried Tomato Lamb

A distinct sun-dried tomato flavour makes this stew a delightful entrée to serve with mashed potatoes or couscous.

All-purpose flour	**3 tbsp.**	**50 mL**
Lamb stew meat	**2 lbs.**	**900 g**
Medium onions, each cut into 8 wedges	**2**	**2**
Medium carrot, chopped	**1**	**1**
Prepared chicken broth	**1 1/2 cups**	**375 mL**
Sun-dried tomatoes in oil, drained and sliced	**1/2 cup**	**125 mL**
Liquid honey	**2 tbsp.**	**30 mL**
Salt	**1/4 tsp.**	**1 mL**
Chopped fresh parsley (or 1 1/2 tsp., 7 mL, flakes)	**2 tbsp.**	**30 mL**

Measure flour into large resealable freezer bag. Add 1/2 of lamb. Seal bag. Toss until coated. Repeat with remaining lamb. Put lamb into 3 1/2 to 4 quart (3.5 to 4 L) slow cooker. Sprinkle with any remaining flour.

Add next 6 ingredients. Stir well. Cover. Cook on Low for 8 to 10 hours or on High for 4 to 5 hours. Skim and discard any fat from surface of liquid in slow cooker.

Add parsley. Stir well. Serves 8.

1 serving: 216 Calories; 7.3 g Total Fat (3.2 g Mono, 0.8 g Poly, 2.4 g Sat); 73 mg Cholesterol; 12 g Carbohydrate; 1 g Fibre; 25 g Protein; 326 mg Sodium

Make Ahead: The night before, cut up onions and carrot. Prepare onion mixture. Chill overnight in covered bowl. Assemble and cook as directed.

Moroccan Lamb Stew

Thick and rich, this warmly spiced stew is best served over couscous or steamed rice.

Medium carrots, cut into 1 inch (2.5 cm) pieces	4	4
Cooking oil	2 tbsp.	30 mL
Lamb stew meat	2 lbs.	900 g
Cooking oil	1 tbsp.	15 mL
Thinly sliced onion	2 cups	500 mL
Garlic cloves, minced (or 1 tsp., 5 mL, powder)	4	4
Ground cumin	2 tsp.	10 mL
Ground coriander	1 tsp.	5 mL
Ground ginger	1 tsp.	5 mL
Ground cinnamon	1/2 tsp.	2 mL
Dried crushed chilies	1/2 tsp.	2 mL
Dry white (or alcohol-free) wine	1/2 cup	125 mL
Orange juice	1/2 cup	125 mL
Brown sugar, packed	1 tbsp.	15 mL
Salt	1/4 tsp.	1 mL
Large pitted green olives, halved (optional)	12	12
Liquid honey	1 tbsp.	15 mL
Grated orange zest	1/2 tsp.	2 mL
Water	1 tbsp.	15 mL
Cornstarch	1 tbsp.	15 mL

Put carrot into 3 1/2 to 4 quart (3.5 to 4 L) slow cooker.

Heat first amount of cooking oil in large frying pan on medium-high. Add lamb in 2 batches. Cook for 8 to 10 minutes per batch, stirring occasionally, until browned. Arrange on top of carrot.

(continued on next page)

Heat second amount of cooking oil in same large frying pan on medium. Add onion. Cook for 5 to 10 minutes, stirring often, until softened.

Add next 6 ingredients. Heat and stir for about 1 minute until fragrant. Scatter over lamb mixture.

Combine next 4 ingredients in 2 cup (500 mL) liquid measure. Pour over lamb mixture. Do not stir. Cover. Cook on Low for 8 to 10 hours or on High for 4 to 5 hours.

Add olives, honey and orange zest. Stir.

Stir water into cornstarch in small cup until smooth. Add to lamb mixture. Stir well. Cover. Cook on High for 5 to 10 minutes until sauce is slightly thickened. Serves 8.

1 serving: *273 Calories; 11.5 g Total Fat (5.5 g Mono, 2.2 g Poly, 2.5 g Sat); 73 mg Cholesterol; 16 g Carbohydrate; 2 g Fibre; 24 g Protein; 167 mg Sodium*

Pictured on page 89.

Make Ahead: The night before, cut up vegetables and olives and prepare wine mixture. Chill overnight in separate covered bowls. Combine spices in small cup. Cover. Assemble and cook as directed.

tip *To slice meat easily, place in freezer for about 30 minutes until just beginning to freeze. If using from frozen state, partially thaw before slicing.*

Sweet Spiced Pork

There's plenty of sweet onion and apple "jus" to serve with this tender pork roast.

Apple juice	**1 cup**	**250 mL**
Applesauce	**1/2 cup**	**125 mL**
Ground coriander	**1 1/2 tbsp.**	**25 mL**
Bay leaves	**2**	**2**
Garlic cloves, minced (or 1/2 tsp., 2 mL, powder)	**2**	**2**
Ground cloves	**1/2 tsp.**	**2 mL**
Dried rosemary, crushed	**1/4 tsp.**	**1 mL**
Salt	**1 tsp.**	**5 mL**
Pepper	**1/2 tsp.**	**2 mL**
Boneless pork shoulder butt roast, trimmed of fat	**3 lbs.**	**1.4 kg**
Sliced onion	**2 cups**	**500 mL**

Combine first 9 ingredients in 2 cup (500 mL) liquid measure. Place roast in large non-metallic bowl. Pour apple juice mixture over top. Turn until coated. Cover. Marinate in refrigerator for at least 6 hours or overnight, turning occasionally.

Put onion into 3 1/2 to 4 quart (3.5 to 4 L) slow cooker. Add roast with marinade. Cover. Cook on Low for 8 to 10 hours. Remove and discard bay leaves. Remove roast to large serving platter. Cover to keep warm. Skim and discard any fat from surface of liquid in slow cooker. Makes about 3 cups (750 mL) jus. Cut roast into thin slices. Serve with jus. Makes 12 servings (2 to 3 oz., 57 to 85 g each, cooked weight).

1 serving: *199 Calories; 7.7 g Total Fat (3.5 g Mono, 0.8 g Poly, 2.6 g Sat); 72 mg Cholesterol; 7 g Carbohydrate; 1 g Fibre; 24 g Protein; 279 mg Sodium*

1. Lamb With Spinach, page 84
2. Moroccan Lamb Stew, page 86

Props Courtesy Of: Danesco Inc.

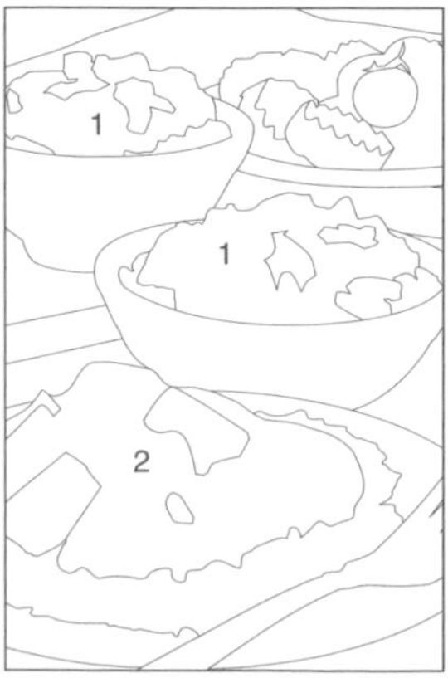

Perfect Pulled Pork

Tender, saucy pork makes a great topping for your favourite rolls. Serve with potato salad and corn on the cob to create a barbecue-style meal indoors!

Boneless pork shoulder butt roast, trimmed of fat	**3 – 4 lbs.**	**1.4 – 1.8 kg**
Apple cider vinegar	**1/2 cup**	**125 mL**
Ketchup	**1/2 cup**	**125 mL**
Fancy (mild) molasses	**1/4 cup**	**60 mL**
Water	**1/4 cup**	**60 mL**
Dijon mustard	**3 tbsp.**	**50 mL**
Worcestershire sauce	**1 tbsp.**	**15 mL**
Pepper	**1 tsp.**	**5 mL**

Place roast in 3 1/2 to 4 quart (3.5 to 4 L) slow cooker.

Combine remaining 7 ingredients in medium bowl. Pour over roast. Cover. Cook on Low for 9 to 10 hours or on High for 4 1/2 to 5 hours. Transfer roast to large plate. Skim and discard any fat from surface of liquid in slow cooker. Shred pork with 2 forks. Return pork to sauce. Stir well. Serves 12.

__1 serving:__ 207 Calories; 7.8 g Total Fat (3.4 g Mono, 1 g Poly, 2.6 g Sat); 72 mg Cholesterol; 9 g Carbohydrate; trace Fibre; 24 g Protein; 275 mg Sodium

Make Ahead: The night before, prepare cider vinegar mixture. Chill overnight in covered bowl. Assemble and cook as directed.

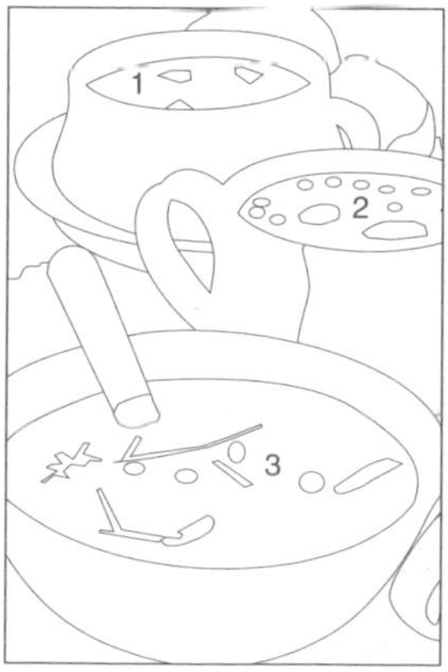

1. Hearty Chicken Soup, page 48
2. Beef Barley Soup, page 21
3. Minestrone, page 101

Props Courtesy Of: Out of the Fire Studio
Scona Clayworks
Treasure Barrel

Mint And Cider Pork

Beautiful pearl onions and colourful baby carrots surround tender pork seasoned with sweet apple cider and a hint of mint.

All-purpose flour	**3 tbsp.**	**50 mL**
Boneless pork shoulder butt roast or steaks, trimmed of fat and cut into 3/4 inch (2 cm) pieces	**2 lbs.**	**900 g**
Cooking oil	**1 tbsp.**	**15 mL**
Baby carrots	**1 lb.**	**454 g**
Tiny white pearl onions, skins removed	**2 cups**	**500 mL**
Apple cider	**1 cup**	**250 mL**
Prepared beef broth	**2/3 cup**	**150 mL**
Salt	**1/4 tsp.**	**1 mL**
Pepper	**1/4 tsp.**	**1 mL**
Frozen peas	**1 cup**	**250 mL**
Chopped fresh mint leaves (or 1 tbsp., 15 mL, dried)	**1/4 cup**	**60 mL**

Measure flour into large resealable freezer bag. Add 1/2 of pork. Seal bag. Toss until coated. Repeat with remaining pork. Heat cooking oil in large frying pan on medium-high. Add pork in 2 batches. Cook for 8 to 10 minutes per batch, stirring occasionally, until browned. Transfer to 3 1/2 to 4 quart (3.5 to 4 L) slow cooker.

Add next 6 ingredients. Stir well. Cover. Cook on Low for 8 to 10 hours or on High for 4 to 5 hours.

Add peas and mint. Stir well. Cover. Cook on High for about 10 minutes until peas are heated through. Serves 8.

1 serving: *265 Calories; 9.5 g Total Fat (4.4 g Mono, 1.4 g Poly, 2.8 g Sat); 71 mg Cholesterol; 18 g Carbohydrate; 3 g Fibre; 26 g Protein; 265 mg Sodium*

Pictured on page 71.

Make Ahead: The night before, cut up pork and prepare vegetables. Chill overnight in separate covered bowls. Assemble and cook as directed.

Pork Goulash

Paprika and tomatoes add deep, rich colour to this thick, savoury sauce. Serve over egg noodles, alongside spaetzle or with mashed potatoes.

All-purpose flour	**1/2 cup**	**125 mL**
Paprika	**4 tsp.**	**20 mL**
Boneless pork shoulder butt steaks, trimmed of fat and cut into 1 inch (2.5 cm) pieces	**3 lbs.**	**1.4 kg**
Cooking oil	**4 tsp.**	**20 mL**
Cooking oil	**2 tsp.**	**10 mL**
Chopped onion	**2 cups**	**500 mL**
Sliced carrot	**2 cups**	**500 mL**
Garlic cloves, minced (or 1 tsp., 5 mL, powder)	**4**	**4**
Caraway seed	**2 tsp.**	**10 mL**
Pepper	**1 tsp.**	**5 mL**
Cans of condensed beef broth (10 oz., 284 mL, each)	**2**	**2**
Tomato paste (see Tip, page 13)	**6 tbsp.**	**100 mL**
Sour cream (or plain yogurt)	**1 cup**	**250 mL**

Combine flour and paprika in large resealable freezer bag. Add 1/2 of pork. Seal bag. Toss until coated. Repeat with remaining pork. Heat first amount of cooking oil in large frying pan on medium. Add pork in 2 batches, reserving any remaining flour mixture. Cook for 5 to 10 minutes per batch, stirring occasionally, until browned. Transfer pork to 4 to 5 quart (4 to 5 L) slow cooker.

Heat second amount of cooking oil in same large frying pan on medium. Add next 5 ingredients. Heat and stir for about 3 minutes, scraping any brown bits from bottom of pan, until onion starts to brown. Add reserved flour mixture. Heat and stir for 1 minute.

Slowly add broth, stirring constantly. Add tomato paste. Heat and stir for about 2 minutes until boiling and thickened. Pour over pork. Do not stir. Cover. Cook on Low for 8 to 10 hours or on High for 4 to 5 hours.

Add sour cream. Stir well. Cover. Heat on High for 1 to 2 minutes until heated through. Serves 12.

***1 serving:** 283 Calories; 13.2 g Total Fat (5.7 g Mono, 1.8 g Poly, 4.7 g Sat); 79 mg Cholesterol; 13 g Carbohydrate; 2 g Fibre; 27 g Protein; 426 mg Sodium*

Make Ahead: The night before, trim and cut up pork and prepare vegetables. Chill overnight in separate covered bowls. Assemble and cook as directed.

Vegetarian Biscuit Stew

Tender vegetables, fragrant with dill, patiently wait beneath a buttermilk biscuit topping for a hungry family. Just add a side salad, and supper is served!

Cooking oil	2 tsp.	10 mL
Thinly sliced onion	2 1/2 cups	625 mL
Thinly sliced celery	1 1/2 cups	375 mL
Garlic cloves, minced (or 1/2 tsp., 2 mL, powder)	2	2
Dried thyme	1 tsp.	5 mL
Pepper	1 tsp.	5 mL
All-purpose flour	2 tbsp.	30 mL
Can of sliced mushrooms (with liquid)	10 oz.	284 mL
Can of condensed cream of mushroom soup	10 oz.	284 mL
Thinly sliced peeled potato	3 cups	750 mL
Thinly sliced carrot	2 cups	500 mL
Thinly sliced parsnip	2 cups	500 mL
Frozen peas	1 cup	250 mL
Tomato juice	1/4 cup	60 mL
Chopped fresh dill (or 1 tbsp., 15 mL, dill weed)	1/4 cup	60 mL
BISCUIT TOPPING		
All-purpose flour	1 1/2 cups	375 mL
Baking powder	1 tbsp.	15 mL
Parsley flakes	2 tsp.	10 mL
Salt	1/2 tsp.	2 mL
Large egg, fork-beaten	1	1
Buttermilk (or reconstituted from powder)	1 cup	250 mL

Heat cooking oil in large frying pan on medium. Add onion and celery. Cook for 5 to 10 minutes, stirring often, until onion is softened.

(continued on next page)

Add garlic, thyme and pepper. Heat and stir for about 1 minute until fragrant.

Add flour. Heat and stir for 1 minute. Add mushrooms and soup. Heat and stir for about 1 minute until boiling and thickened. Transfer to 4 to 5 quart (4 to 5 L) slow cooker.

Add potato, carrot and parsnip. Stir well. Cover. Cook on Low for 8 to 9 hours or on High for 4 to 4 1/2 hours.

Add peas, tomato juice and dill. Stir well. Cover.

Biscuit Topping: Combine first 4 ingredients in medium bowl. Make a well in centre.

Add egg and buttermilk to well. Stir until just moistened. Spoon batter evenly on top of vegetable mixture. Cover. Cook on High for 30 to 40 minutes until wooden pick inserted in centre of topping comes out clean. Serves 6.

__1 serving:__ 411 Calories; 7.6 g Total Fat (2.2 g Mono, 2.8 g Poly, 1.8 g Sat); 38 mg Cholesterol; 75 g Carbohydrate; 9 g Fibre; 13 g Protein; 1090 mg Sodium

Make Ahead: The night before, prepare and assemble first 12 ingredients, as directed, in slow cooker liner. Cover. Chill overnight. Cook as directed.

tip *To reduce the heat in chili peppers and jalapeño peppers, remove the seeds and ribs. Wear rubber gloves and avoid touching your eyes when handling hot peppers. Wash your hands well afterwards.*

Herbed Barley Risotto

A flavourful risotto made with barley instead of rice.

Cooking oil	1 tbsp.	15 mL
Finely chopped onion	1 cup	250 mL
Sliced fresh white mushrooms	2 cups	500 mL
Garlic cloves, minced (or 1 tsp., 5 mL, powder)	4	4
Prepared vegetable broth	2 2/3 cups	650 mL
Medium tomatoes, peeled (see Tip, page 105), quartered, seeds removed	3	3
Pearl barley, rinsed and drained	1 cup	250 mL
Dry white (or alcohol-free) wine	1/2 cup	125 mL
Dried whole oregano	1/2 tsp.	2 mL
Dried rosemary, crushed	1/2 tsp.	2 mL
Salt	1/4 tsp.	1 mL
Pepper	1/4 tsp.	1 mL
Grated Parmesan cheese	1/3 cup	75 mL
Chopped fresh parsley (or 1 1/2 tsp., 7 mL, flakes)	2 tbsp.	30 mL

Heat cooking oil in medium frying pan on medium. Add onion. Cook for 5 to 10 minutes, stirring often, until softened.

Add mushrooms and garlic. Cook for 3 to 5 minutes, stirring occasionally, until mushrooms are softened. Transfer to 3 1/2 to 4 quart (3.5 to 4 L) slow cooker.

Add next 8 ingredients. Stir well. Cover. Cook on Low for 8 to 9 hours or on High for 4 to 4 1/2 hours.

Add Parmesan cheese and parsley. Stir well. Serves 4.

1 serving: *341 Calories; 7.7 g Total Fat (3.1 g Mono, 1.6 g Poly, 2.3 g Sat); 7 mg Cholesterol; 53 g Carbohydrate; 7 g Fibre; 13 g Protein; 882 mg Sodium*

Make Ahead: The night before, slice mushrooms and prepare tomato mixture. Chill overnight in separate covered bowls. Assemble and cook as directed.

Curried Cauliflower Soup

A classic combination of cauliflower and curry makes a colourful, spicy soup. Dare to make something deliciously different for dinner!

Cooking oil	1 tbsp.	15 mL
Chopped onion	1 1/2 cups	375 mL
Chopped carrot	1 cup	250 mL
Chopped celery	1 cup	250 mL
Curry paste	2 tbsp.	30 mL
Garlic cloves, minced (or 1/2 tsp., 2 mL, powder)	2	2
Prepared vegetable broth	5 cups	1.25 L
Medium potatoes, peeled, cubed	2	2
Salt	1/4 tsp.	1 mL
Chopped cauliflower	2 1/2 cups	625 mL
Plain yogurt	1/2 cup	125 mL
Chopped fresh cilantro or parsley (or 1 1/2 tsp., 7 mL, dried)	2 tbsp.	30 mL

Heat cooking oil in large frying pan on medium. Add next 3 ingredients. Cook for 5 to 10 minutes, stirring often, until onion is softened.

Add curry paste and garlic. Heat and stir for about 1 minute until fragrant. Transfer to 4 to 5 quart (4 to 5 L) slow cooker.

Add next 3 ingredients. Stir well. Cover. Cook on Low for 8 to 10 hours or on High for 4 to 5 hours. Carefully process with hand blender or in blender until smooth.

Add cauliflower and yogurt. Stir well. Cover. Cook on High for about 45 minutes until cauliflower is tender-crisp.

Add cilantro. Stir. Makes about 8 cups (2 L).

***1 cup (250 mL):** 108 Calories; 3.9 g Total Fat (1.9 g Mono, 1 g Poly, 0.6 g Sat); 1 mg Cholesterol; 15 g Carbohydrate; 3 g Fibre; 5 g Protein; 644 mg Sodium*

Acorn Apple Soup

As golden as the harvest fields, this sweet 'n' spicy blend of autumn flavours is simply sensational.

Acorn squash, chopped (about 8 cups, 2 L), reserving 1/2 cup (125 mL) seeds	**2 1/2 lbs.**	**1.1 kg**
Tart medium cooking apples (such as Granny Smith), peeled and cores removed, chopped	**4**	**4**
Prepared chicken broth	**3 cups**	**750 mL**
Chopped peeled potato	**1 cup**	**250 mL**
Applesauce	**1/2 cup**	**125 mL**
Chopped onion	**1/2 cup**	**125 mL**
Bay leaves	**2**	**2**
Finely grated, peeled gingerroot	**1 tbsp.**	**15 mL**
Ground nutmeg	**1/4 tsp.**	**1 mL**
Cooking oil	**1 tsp.**	**5 mL**
Salt	**1/8 tsp.**	**0.5 mL**
Reserved acorn squash seeds, rinsed and dried	**1/2 cup**	**125 mL**

Combine first 9 ingredients in 5 to 7 quart (5 to 7 L) slow cooker. Cover. Cook on Low for 8 to 10 hours or on High for 4 to 5 hours. Remove and discard bay leaves. Carefully process with hand blender or in blender until smooth. Makes about 9 cups (2.25 L) soup.

Combine cooking oil and salt in medium bowl. Add squash seeds. Toss until coated. Spread evenly in ungreased shallow pan. Bake in 300°F (150°C) oven for about 20 minutes, stirring or shaking often, until crisp and golden. Divide and ladle soup into 6 individual bowls. Sprinkle each with toasted seeds. Serves 6.

***1 serving:** 212 Calories; 3.1 g Total Fat (1.1 g Mono, 1 g Poly, 0.6 g Sat); 0 mg Cholesterol; 44 g Carbohydrate; 6 g Fibre; 6 g Protein; 471 mg Sodium*

Make Ahead: The night before, combine first 9 ingredients in slow cooker liner. Cover. Chill overnight. Seeds may be prepared the night before and stored in covered bowl. Cook as directed.

Zesty Southwestern Soup

Turn up the heat with a steaming bowl of this spicy soup. Serve with tortilla chips instead of crackers.

Prepared vegetable broth	**5 cups**	**1.25 L**
Diced peeled potato	**2 2/3 cups**	**650 mL**
Thinly sliced onion	**1 3/4 cups**	**425 mL**
Thinly sliced celery	**1 cup**	**250 mL**
Can of diced green chilies (with juice)	**4 oz.**	**113 g**
Roma (plum) tomatoes, seeds removed, chopped	**2**	**2**
Garlic cloves, minced (or 1/2 tsp., 2 mL, powder)	**2**	**2**
Chili powder	**1 tsp.**	**5 mL**
Ground cumin	**1 tsp.**	**5 mL**
Cayenne pepper	**1/2 tsp.**	**2 mL**
Grated sharp Cheddar cheese	**1 cup**	**250 mL**
Medium salsa, for garnish		
Chopped fresh cilantro or parsley (or 3/4 tsp., 4 mL, dried), for garnish		

Combine first 10 ingredients in 3 1/2 to 4 quart (3.5 to 4 L) slow cooker. Cover. Cook on Low for 8 to 10 hours or on High for 4 to 5 hours. Carefully process with hand blender or in blender until smooth.

Add cheese. Stir until cheese is melted.

Garnish individual servings with salsa and cilantro. Makes about 6 1/2 cups (1.6 L).

1 cup (250 mL): *176 Calories; 7 g Total Fat (1.9 g Mono, 0.3 g Poly, 4.2 g Sat); 19 mg Cholesterol; 20 g Carbohydrate; 3 g Fibre; 10 g Protein; 985 mg Sodium*

Make Ahead: The night before, combine first 10 ingredients in slow cooker liner. Cover. Chill overnight. Cook as directed.

tip *To bruise cardamom, hit cardamom pods with mallet or flat side of wide knife to "bruise" or crack them slightly open.*

Spicy Beans And Rice

Serve with tortilla chips and crisp vegetables.
Great topped with a dollop of sour cream and a spoonful of salsa.

Can of red kidney beans, rinsed and drained	**19 oz.**	**540 mL**
Prepared vegetable broth	**1 1/4 cups**	**300 mL**
Chopped red pepper	**1 cup**	**250 mL**
Chopped tomato	**1 cup**	**250 mL**
Chopped onion	**1 cup**	**250 mL**
Chopped celery	**1/2 cup**	**125 mL**
Chipotle chili pepper, chopped (see Tip, page 95)	**1**	**1**
Curry powder	**2 tsp.**	**10 mL**
Dried whole oregano	**1 tsp.**	**5 mL**
Salt	**1/2 tsp.**	**2 mL**
Pepper	**1/4 tsp.**	**1 mL**
Converted white (or brown) rice	**1/2 cup**	**125 mL**
Chopped green onion	**1/3 cup**	**75 mL**
Chopped fresh parsley (or 1 1/2 tsp., 7 mL, flakes)	**2 tbsp.**	**30 mL**
Lime juice	**1 tbsp.**	**15 mL**

Combine first 11 ingredients in 3 1/2 to 4 quart (3.5 to 4 L) slow cooker. Cover. Cook on Low for 8 to 9 hours or on High for 4 to 4 1/2 hours.

Add rice. Stir well. Cover. Cook on High for 30 to 45 minutes until rice is tender. Add remaining 3 ingredients. Stir gently. Serves 4.

__1 serving:__ 228 Calories; 1.2 g Total Fat (0.2 g Mono, 0.4 g Poly, 0.2 g Sat); 0 mg Cholesterol; 46 g Carbohydrate; 7 g Fibre; 10 g Protein; 731 mg Sodium

Pictured on page 107.

Make Ahead: The night before, combine first 11 ingredients in slow cooker liner. Cover. Chill overnight. Cook as directed.

EASY BURRITOS: Spoon about 1/2 cup (125 mL) Spicy Beans And Rice down centre of each of eight 9 inch (22 cm) flour tortillas. Layer chopped or torn lettuce, sour cream, salsa, grated Cheddar cheese and chopped tomato on top of each. Fold sides of tortillas over filling. Roll up each from bottom to enclose filling.

Pictured on page 107.

Minestrone

A large quantity recipe that will fill your slow cooker with a nourishing tomato and cabbage soup the whole family will enjoy!

Prepared chicken (or vegetable) broth	**6 cups**	**1.5 L**
Cans of diced tomatoes (with juice), 14 oz. (398 mL) each	**2**	**2**
Can of white kidney beans, rinsed and drained	**19 oz.**	**540 mL**
Shredded cabbage, lightly packed	**2 cups**	**500 mL**
Sliced celery	**1 3/4 cups**	**425 mL**
Diced carrot	**1 3/4 cups**	**425 mL**
Medium leeks (white part only), cut in half lengthwise, thinly sliced	**3**	**3**
Garlic cloves, minced (or 1/2 tsp., 2 mL, powder)	**2**	**2**
Granulated sugar	**1 tsp.**	**5 mL**
Dried basil	**1/2 tsp.**	**2 mL**
Salt	**1/2 tsp.**	**2 mL**
Pepper	**1/2 tsp.**	**2 mL**
Diced zucchini (with peel)	**1 cup**	**250 mL**
Frozen cut green beans, thawed	**1 cup**	**250 mL**
Grated Parmesan cheese, for garnish		

Combine first 12 ingredients in 5 to 7 quart (5 to 7 L) slow cooker. Cover. Cook on Low for 9 to 10 hours or on High for 4 1/2 to 5 hours.

Add zucchini and green beans. Stir well. Cover. Cook on High for about 20 minutes until green beans are tender.

Garnish individual servings with Parmesan cheese. Makes about 15 cups (3.74 L).

1 cup (250 mL): *84 Calories; 1 g Total Fat (0.3 g Mono, 0.3 g Poly, 0.2 g Sat); 0 mg Cholesterol; 15 g Carbohydrate; 3 g Fibre; 5 g Protein; 568 mg Sodium*

Pictured on page 90.

Make Ahead: The night before, combine first 12 ingredients in slow cooker liner. Cover. Chill overnight. Cook as directed.

Lentil Rice Rolls

Flavours of the world unite in these interesting cabbage rolls. Definitely worth a try when you're looking for something a bit different.

Medium head of green cabbage (about 3 lbs., 1.4 kg)	**1**	**1**
Boiling water		
Can of lentils, rinsed and drained	**19 oz.**	**540 mL**
Can of tomato sauce	**7 1/2 oz.**	**213 mL**
Long grain brown (or white) rice	**1/2 cup**	**125 mL**
Finely chopped carrot	**1/2 cup**	**125 mL**
Finely chopped celery	**1/2 cup**	**125 mL**
Finely chopped onion	**1/2 cup**	**125 mL**
Garlic clove, minced (or 1/4 tsp., 1 mL, powder)	**1**	**1**
Dried whole oregano	**1/2 tsp.**	**2 mL**
Can of tomato sauce	**25 oz.**	**680 mL**
Dark raisins	**1/4 cup**	**60 mL**
Lemon juice	**3 tbsp.**	**50 mL**
Brown sugar, packed	**2 tbsp.**	**30 mL**
Grated lemon zest	**2 tsp.**	**10 mL**
Ground cinnamon	**1/2 tsp.**	**2 mL**

Remove 10 larger outer leaves from cabbage head. Place leaves in large bowl. Add boiling water until 2 inches (5 cm) above leaves. Let stand for about 5 minutes until softened. Cut 'V' shape with knife along tough ribs of cabbage leaves to remove. Discard ribs. Set leaves aside. Shred remaining cabbage. Put into 5 to 7 quart (5 to 7 L) slow cooker.

Combine next 8 ingredients in large bowl. Spoon about 1/3 cup (75 mL) lentil mixture onto centre of each cabbage leaf. Fold sides of leaves over filling. Roll up each tightly from bottom to enclose filling. Makes 10 cabbage rolls.

Measure remaining 6 ingredients into medium bowl. Stir. Add 1 1/2 cups (375 mL) tomato sauce mixture to shredded cabbage in slow cooker. Stir well. Spread evenly in slow cooker. Arrange rolls, seam-side down, on top of cabbage mixture. Pour remaining tomato sauce mixture on top of rolls. Cover. Cook on Low for 8 to 10 hours or on High for 4 to 5 hours. Carefully transfer rolls to large plate. Remove cabbage mixture to large serving platter. Arrange rolls on top. Serves 10.

(continued on next page)

1 serving: *151 Calories; 0.9 g Total Fat (0.2 g Mono, 0.4 g Poly, 0.1 g Sat); 0 mg Cholesterol; 33 g Carbohydrate; 5 g Fibre; 6 g Protein; 654 mg Sodium*

Make Ahead: The night before, prepare and assemble all ingredients, as directed, in slow cooker liner. Cover. Chill overnight. Cook as directed.

Cauliflower Dhal

Dinner's ready, DAHL-ings! Treat the ones you love to this spicy, traditional East Indian dish. Perfect with pappadum, an East Indian flatbread.

Cauliflower florets	**4 cups**	**1 L**
Chopped peeled potato	**2 cups**	**500 mL**
Yellow split peas, rinsed and drained	**1 cup**	**250 mL**
Chopped onion	**1 cup**	**250 mL**
Garlic clove, minced (or 1/4 tsp., 1 mL, powder)	**1**	**1**
Prepared vegetable broth	**3 cups**	**750 mL**
Balsamic vinegar	**2 tbsp.**	**30 mL**
Red curry paste	**1 tsp.**	**5 mL**
Turmeric	**1/4 tsp.**	**1 mL**
Ground ginger	**1/4 tsp.**	**1 mL**
Ground nutmeg	**1/4 tsp.**	**1 mL**
Salt	**1/2 tsp.**	**2 mL**
Pepper	**1/2 tsp.**	**2 mL**

Combine first 5 ingredients in 4 to 5 quart (4 to 5 L) slow cooker.

Measure remaining 8 ingredients into medium bowl. Stir well. Pour over cauliflower mixture. Stir well. Cover. Cook on Low for 8 to 9 hours or on High for 4 to 4 1/2 hours. Makes about 7 1/2 cups (1.9 L).

1 cup (250 mL): *101 Calories; 0.8 g Total Fat (0.2 g Mono, 0.2 g Poly, 0.2 g Sat); 0 mg Cholesterol; 19 g Carbohydrate; 3 g Fibre; 6 g Protein; 575 mg Sodium*

Make Ahead: The night before, prepare and assemble all 13 ingredients, as directed, in slow cooker liner. Cover. Chill overnight. Cook as directed.

Paré Pointer

They tried to return their chimp to the pet store but found there was a no monkey-back guarantee.

Yam And Spinach Pasta

"Pasta yam and spinach, please!" will be music to your ears when you serve this savoury dish the whole family will love. Add a little milk or cream if you like a thinner sauce.

Hard margarine (or butter)	1 tbsp.	15 mL
Chopped onion	1 cup	250 mL
Sliced fresh white mushrooms	1 1/2 cups	375 mL
Garlic cloves, minced (or 1/2 tsp., 2 mL, powder)	2	2
Hard margarine (or butter)	1 tbsp.	15 mL
All-purpose flour	2 tbsp.	30 mL
Prepared vegetable broth	1 cup	250 mL
Dry white (or alcohol-free) wine	1/2 cup	125 mL
Chopped yam	3 cups	750 mL
Chopped fresh rosemary leaves (or 1/4 tsp., 1 mL, dried, crushed)	1 tsp.	5 mL
Salt	1/4 tsp.	1 mL
Pepper	1/4 tsp.	1 mL
Fresh spinach, stems removed, lightly packed	2 cups	500 mL
Prepared vegetable broth	1/2 cup	125 mL
Chopped green onion	1/3 cup	75 mL
Sour cream	1/4 cup	60 mL
Dijon mustard (with whole seeds)	1 tbsp.	15 mL
Penne pasta (about 6 oz., 170 g)	2 cups	500 mL
Boiling water	10 cups	2.5 L
Salt	1 1/4 tsp.	6 mL
Grated Parmesan cheese	1/3 cup	75 mL

Melt first amount of margarine in medium frying pan on medium. Add onion. Cook for 5 to 10 minutes, stirring often, until softened.

(continued on next page)

Add mushrooms and garlic. Cook for 3 to 5 minutes, stirring occasionally, until mushrooms are softened. Transfer to 3 1/2 to 4 quart (3.5 to 4 L) slow cooker.

Melt second amount of margarine in same medium frying pan on medium. Add flour. Heat and stir for 1 minute. Slowly add first amount of broth, stirring constantly until smooth. Add wine. Heat and stir for about 3 minutes until boiling and thickened. Add to mushroom mixture. Stir.

Add next 4 ingredients. Stir well. Cover. Cook on Low for 6 to 7 hours or on High for 3 to 3 1/2 hours. Mash yam slightly.

Add next 5 ingredients. Stir well. Cover. Cook on High for about 10 minutes until spinach is wilted.

Cook pasta in boiling water and second amount of salt in large uncovered pot or Dutch oven for 8 to 10 minutes, stirring occasionally, until tender but firm. Drain. Return pasta to pot. Add yam mixture. Toss until coated.

Add Parmesan cheese. Stir gently. Serves 6.

***1 serving:** 361 Calories; 8.3 g Total Fat (3.6 g Mono, 1 g Poly, 3 g Sat); 9 mg Cholesterol; 58 g Carbohydrate; 6 g Fibre; 11 g Protein; 528 mg Sodium*

Make Ahead: The night before, prepare and assemble first 12 ingredients, as directed, in slow cooker liner. Cover. Chill overnight. Cook as directed.

tip *To peel tomatoes, cut an X just through skin on bottom of tomato. Plunge into boiling water for 30 seconds, then immediately into bowl of ice cold water. Peel skin.*

Vegetable Curry

A colourful combination of chickpeas and vegetables, seasoned with a mellow blend of ginger, curry and coconut milk.

Can of coconut milk	**14 oz.**	**398 mL**
Curry paste	**2 tbsp.**	**30 mL**
All-purpose flour	**1 1/2 tbsp.**	**25 mL**
Cauliflower florets	**3 cups**	**750 mL**
Chopped peeled potato	**3 cups**	**750 mL**
Can of chickpeas (garbanzo beans), rinsed and drained	**19 oz.**	**540 mL**
Chopped carrot	**2 cups**	**500 mL**
Chopped onion	**1 2/3 cups**	**400 mL**
Finely grated, peeled gingerroot	**1 tbsp.**	**15 mL**
Garlic cloves, minced (or 1/2 tsp., 2 mL, powder)	**2**	**2**
Frozen peas	**1/2 cup**	**125 mL**

Beat first 3 ingredients with whisk in extra-large bowl until smooth.

Add next 7 ingredients. Stir well. Transfer to 5 to 7 quart (5 to 7 L) slow cooker. Cover. Cook on Low for 7 to 8 hours or on High for 3 1/2 to 4 hours.

Add peas. Stir gently. Cover. Cook on High for 5 to 10 minutes until peas are heated through. Serves 8.

1 serving: *261 Calories; 12.7 g Total Fat (1.3 g Mono, 0.9 g Poly, 9.3 g Sat); 0 mg Cholesterol; 33 g Carbohydrate; 5 g Fibre; 7 g Protein; 133 mg Sodium*

Make Ahead: The night before, prepare and assemble first 10 ingredients, as directed, in slow cooker liner. Cover. Chill overnight. Cook as directed.

1. Easy Burritos, page 100
2. Spicy Beans And Rice, page 100

Props Courtesy Of: Hamilton Beach® Canada
Pier 1 Imports

KEEP WARM
LOW

Root Soup

A back-to-basics broth and vegetable soup with a sweet, earthy flavour. Delicious with whole grain bread. Make when celeriac (celery root) is in season.

Prepared vegetable broth	**8 cups**	**2 L**
Medium potatoes, peeled, chopped	**3**	**3**
Chopped onion	**3 cups**	**750 mL**
Chopped peeled celeriac (celery root)	**2 cups**	**500 mL**
Chopped carrot	**2 cups**	**500 mL**
Chopped yam (or sweet potato)	**2 cups**	**500 mL**
Medium parsnip, chopped	**1**	**1**
Salt	**1/4 tsp.**	**1 mL**
Pepper	**1/4 tsp.**	**1 mL**

Combine all 9 ingredients in 5 to 7 quart (5 to 7 L) slow cooker. Cover. Cook on Low for 8 to 10 hours or on High for 4 to 5 hours. Carefully process with hand blender or in blender until smooth. Makes about 11 cups (2.75 L).

1 cup (250 mL): *120 Calories; 0.7 g Total Fat (0.2 g Mono, 0.1 g Poly, 0.2 g Sat); 0 mg Cholesterol; 25 g Carbohydrate; 4 g Fibre; 5 g Protein; 712 mg Sodium*

Make Ahead: The night before, combine all 9 ingredients in slow cooker liner. Cover. Chill overnight. Cook as directed.

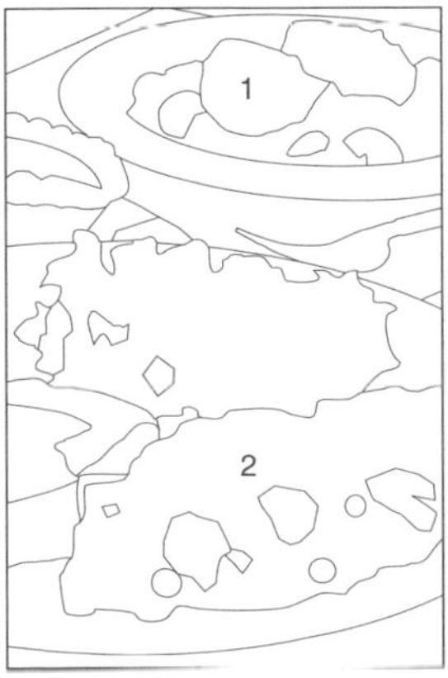

1. Squash And Dumplings, page 114
2. Squash And Lentil Curry, page 113

Props Courtesy Of: Emile Henry
Pfaltzgraff Canada

Creamy Cauliflower Rotini

A little spice is always nice! Use less jalapeño pepper, if desired, to cut the heat of this creamy, cheesy dish. Sauce freezes well to reheat and add to pasta another day.

Cauliflower florets	3 cups	750 mL
Prepared vegetable broth	3 cups	750 mL
Can of white kidney beans, rinsed and drained	19 oz.	540 mL
Chopped red pepper	1 cup	250 mL
Chopped carrot	1 cup	250 mL
Finely chopped onion	1 cup	250 mL
Ground cumin	1 tsp.	5 mL
Chili powder	1 tsp.	5 mL
Salt	1/4 tsp.	1 mL
Pepper	1/4 tsp.	1 mL
All-purpose flour	2 tbsp.	30 mL
Grated white Cheddar cheese	1 cup	250 mL
Frozen peas	1 cup	250 mL
Block of cream cheese, cut up, softened	4 oz.	125 g
Finely chopped canned jalapeño pepper	2 tbsp.	30 mL
Rotini pasta (about 24 oz., 681 g)	9 cups	2.25 L
Boiling water	24 cups	6 L
Salt	1 tbsp.	15 mL

Combine first 10 ingredients in 4 to 5 quart (4 to 5 L) slow cooker. Cover. Cook on Low for 8 to 9 hours or on High for 4 to 4 1/2 hours.

Measure flour into small bowl. Add Cheddar cheese. Toss until coated. Add to cauliflower mixture. Stir.

Add next 3 ingredients. Stir well. Cover. Cook on High for about 30 minutes until sauce is slightly thickened.

Cook pasta in boiling water and second amount of salt in large uncovered pot or Dutch oven for 10 to 12 minutes, stirring occasionally, until tender but firm. Drain. Return pasta to pot. Add cauliflower mixture. Toss until coated. Serves 8.

(continued on next page)

1 serving: 535 Calories; 12.5 g Total Fat (3.2 g Mono, 1.1 g Poly, 7 g Sat); 33 mg Cholesterol; 83 g Carbohydrate; 8 g Fibre; 22 g Protein; 682 mg Sodium

Make Ahead: The night before, combine first 10 ingredients in slow cooker liner. Cover. Chill overnight. Cook as directed.

Fall Bounty Soup

Vegetables aplenty in this thick, hearty soup topped with French bread and golden cheese. You've just "gouda" try it!

Prepared vegetable broth	**4 cups**	**1 L**
Diced sweet potato (or yam)	**2 cups**	**500 mL**
Chopped cauliflower	**2 cups**	**500 mL**
Diced peeled potato	**1 cup**	**250 mL**
Chopped carrot	**1 cup**	**250 mL**
Chopped onion	**1 cup**	**250 mL**
Bay leaf	**1**	**1**
Granulated sugar	**1 tsp.**	**5 mL**
Dried thyme	**1/2 tsp.**	**2 mL**
Salt	**1/2 tsp.**	**2 mL**
Pepper	**1/2 tsp.**	**2 mL**
French bread slices, 1/2 inch (12 mm) thick	**6**	**6**
Grated Gouda cheese	**1 cup**	**250 mL**

Combine first 11 ingredients in 3 1/2 to 4 quart (3.5 to 4 L) slow cooker. Cover. Cook on Low for 8 to 10 hours or on High for 4 to 5 hours. Remove and discard bay leaf. Makes about 6 1/2 cups (1.6 L) soup.

Arrange bread slices on ungreased baking sheet. Sprinkle each with 2 1/2 tbsp. (37 mL) cheese. Broil 4 inches (10 cm) from heat in oven for 2 to 3 minutes until cheese is melted and golden. Divide and ladle soup into 6 individual bowls. Top each with 1 bread slice. Serves 6.

1 serving: 250 Calories; 7.8 g Total Fat (2.2 g Mono, 0.5 g Poly, 4.6 g Sat); 27 mg Cholesterol; 34 g Carbohydrate; 4 g Fibre; 12 g Protein; 1087 mg Sodium

Make Ahead: The night before, combine first 11 ingredients in slow cooker liner. Cover. Chill overnight. Cook as directed.

Rice And Bean Tacos

Hearty, meatless taco filling with a slight nuttiness from the wild rice. Topped with sour cream, lettuce and cheese, these look great on a finger food buffet. Take them to your next potluck!

RICE AND BEAN FILLING		
Cans of mixed beans (19 oz., 540 mL, each), rinsed and drained	**2**	**2**
Can of diced tomatoes (with juice)	**28 oz.**	**796 mL**
Prepared vegetable broth	**1 cup**	**250 mL**
Wild rice	**1/2 cup**	**125 mL**
Can of diced green chilies	**4 oz.**	**113 g**
Chili powder	**2 tsp.**	**10 mL**
Granulated sugar	**1 tsp.**	**5 mL**
Ground cumin	**1 tsp.**	**5 mL**
Dried whole oregano	**1 tsp.**	**5 mL**
Pepper	**1/2 tsp.**	**2 mL**
Taco shells	**24**	**24**
Sour cream (optional)	**1 cup**	**250 mL**
Chopped or torn lettuce	**1 1/2 cups**	**375 mL**
Grated medium Cheddar cheese	**1 1/2 cups**	**375 mL**

Rice And Bean Filling: Combine first 10 ingredients in 3 1/2 to 4 quart (3.5 to 4 L) slow cooker. Cover. Cook on Low for 8 to 10 hours or on High for 4 to 5 hours. Makes about 6 cups (1.5 L) filling.

Heat taco shells according to package directions. Spoon 1/4 cup (60 mL) filling into each shell.

Spoon 2 tsp. (10 mL) sour cream over filling in each shell. Divide and sprinkle lettuce and cheese over sour cream. Makes 24 tacos.

1 taco: *141 Calories; 5.8 g Total Fat (2 g Mono, 1.4 g Poly, 2.1 g Sat); 8 mg Cholesterol; 18 g Carbohydrate; 3 g Fibre; 6 g Protein; 291 mg Sodium*

Pictured on front cover.

Make Ahead: The night before, combine first 10 ingredients in slow cooker liner. Cover. Chill overnight. Cook as directed.

Squash And Lentil Curry

A thick, mildly spiced lentil and vegetable curry—a fusion of fantastic flavours. Serve with flatbread and crisp salad.

Prepared vegetable broth	**3 cups**	**750 mL**
Chopped onion	**1 1/2 cups**	**375 mL**
All-purpose flour	**2 tbsp.**	**30 mL**
Curry paste	**2 tbsp.**	**30 mL**
Garlic cloves, minced (or 1/2 tsp., 2 mL, powder)	**2**	**2**
Pepper	**1/4 tsp.**	**1 mL**
Chopped butternut squash	**2 cups**	**500 mL**
Dried green lentils, rinsed and drained	**1 1/4 cups**	**300 mL**
Chopped yam (or sweet potato)	**1 cup**	**250 mL**
Fresh spinach, stems removed, lightly packed	**3 cups**	**750 mL**
Frozen peas	**1 cup**	**250 mL**
Plain yogurt	**1/3 cup**	**75 mL**
Raw cashews, toasted (see Tip, page 39)	**1/3 cup**	**75 mL**
Salt, just a pinch		

Combine first 6 ingredients in 3 1/2 to 4 quart (3.5 to 4 L) slow cooker.

Add squash, lentils and yam. Stir well. Cover. Cook on Low for 7 to 8 hours or on High for 3 1/2 to 4 hours.

Add spinach and peas. Stir gently. Cover. Cook on High for 5 to 10 minutes until spinach is wilted and peas are heated through.

Add remaining 3 ingredients. Stir gently. Serves 6.

1 serving: *334 Calories; 6.8 g Total Fat (3.4 g Mono, 1.5 g Poly, 1.3 g Sat); 1 mg Cholesterol; 53 g Carbohydrate; 10 g Fibre; 19 g Protein; 488 mg Sodium*

Pictured on page 108.

Make Ahead: The night before, assemble first 9 ingredients, as directed, in slow cooker liner. Cover. Chill overnight. Cook as directed.

Squash And Dumplings

A subtly spiced, meatless stew topped with cheesy cornmeal dumplings. Enticing Italian flavour and a variety of textures make this dish particularly pleasing!

Butternut squash, cut into 1/2 inch (12 mm) pieces (about 3 cups, 750 mL)	**3/4 lb.**	**340 g**
Cans of Italian-style stewed tomatoes (14 oz., 398 mL, each)	**2**	**2**
Can of mixed beans, rinsed and drained	**19 oz.**	**540 mL**
Small fresh white mushrooms, halved	**2 cups**	**500 mL**
Water	**1 cup**	**250 mL**
Garlic cloves, minced (or 1/2 tsp., 2 mL, powder)	**2**	**2**
Italian seasoning	**2 tsp.**	**10 mL**
Pepper	**1/4 tsp.**	**1 mL**

CORNMEAL DUMPLINGS

All-purpose flour	**1/2 cup**	**125 mL**
Yellow cornmeal	**1/3 cup**	**75 mL**
Grated Parmesan cheese	**2 tbsp.**	**30 mL**
Baking powder	**1 tsp.**	**5 mL**
Paprika	**1/8 tsp.**	**0.5 mL**
Large egg	**1**	**1**
Milk	**2 tbsp.**	**30 mL**
Cooking oil	**2 tbsp.**	**30 mL**
Basil pesto	**1 tsp.**	**5 mL**

Combine first 8 ingredients in 4 to 5 quart (4 to 5 L) slow cooker. Cover. Cook on Low for 8 to 9 hours or on High for 4 to 4 1/2 hours.

Cornmeal Dumplings: Measure first 5 ingredients into medium bowl. Stir. Make a well in centre.

Beat remaining 4 ingredients with fork in small cup. Add to well. Stir until just moistened. Spoon mounds of batter, using 2 tbsp. (30 mL) for each, in single layer on top of squash mixture. Cover. Cook on High for 40 to 50 minutes until wooden pick inserted in centre of dumpling comes out clean. Serves 6.

(continued on next page)

1 serving: *273 Calories; 7.5 g Total Fat (3.5 g Mono, 2 g Poly, 1.2 g Sat); 38 mg Cholesterol; 45 g Carbohydrate; 6 g Fibre; 10 g Protein; 742 mg Sodium*

Pictured on page 108.

Make Ahead: The night before, combine first 8 ingredients in slow cooker liner. Cover. Chill overnight. Cook as directed.

Chili Black Beans

A colourful, spicy blend of veggies and beans. Add a dollop of sour cream or salsa and sprinkle with green onion or cilantro, if desired.

Cans of black beans (19 oz., 540 mL, each), rinsed and drained	**2**	**2**
Chopped butternut squash	**2 cups**	**500 mL**
Can of diced tomatoes (with juice)	**14 oz.**	**398 mL**
Chopped onion	**1 1/2 cups**	**375 mL**
Prepared vegetable broth	**1/2 cup**	**125 mL**
Jalapeño pepper (with seeds), finely diced (see Tip, page 95)	**1**	**1**
Chili powder	**1 tbsp.**	**15 mL**
Bay leaves	**2**	**2**
Garlic cloves, minced (or 1/2 tsp., 2 mL, powder)	**2**	**2**
Salt	**1/4 tsp.**	**1 mL**
Chopped green pepper	**1 cup**	**250 mL**

Combine first 10 ingredients in 3 1/2 to 4 quart (3.5 to 4 L) slow cooker. Cover. Cook on Low for 8 to 10 hours or on High for 4 to 5 hours.

Add green pepper. Stir gently. Cover. Cook on High for about 20 minutes until green pepper is tender-crisp. Remove and discard bay leaves. Serves 6.

1 serving: *183 Calories; 1.1 g Total Fat (0.1 g Mono, 0.4 g Poly, 0.2 g Sat); 0 mg Cholesterol; 36 g Carbohydrate; 6 g Fibre; 10 g Protein; 504 mg Sodium*

Pictured on page 144.

Make Ahead: The night before, combine first 10 ingredients in slow cooker liner. Cover. Chill overnight. Cook as directed.

Chunky Vegetable Chili

Colourful, chunky chili loaded with a variety of tender veggies. Cheddar cheese garnish adds just the right touch. Serve with buns or salad.

Medium carrots, cut into 1 inch (2.5 cm) pieces	4	4
Celery ribs, cut into 1 inch (2.5 cm) pieces	4	4
Medium onions, cut into 1 inch (2.5 cm) pieces	2	2
Large green pepper, seeds and ribs removed, cut into 1 inch (2.5 cm) pieces	1	1
Can of chickpeas (garbanzo beans), rinsed and drained	19 oz.	540 mL
Can of baby corn, drained	14 oz.	398 mL
Can of diced tomatoes, drained and juice reserved	14 oz.	398 mL
Tomato paste (see Tip, page 13)	1/3 cup	75 mL
Reserved juice from tomatoes	1/3 cup	75 mL
Medium salsa	1/3 cup	75 mL
Chili powder	1 1/2 – 2 tsp.	7 – 10 mL
Ground cumin	1 – 1 1/2 tsp.	5 – 7 mL
Dried whole oregano	1/2 – 1 tsp.	2 – 5 mL
Salt	1/2 tsp.	2 mL
Pepper	1/2 tsp.	2 mL
Small zucchini (with peel), halved lengthwise, cut into 1 inch (2.5 cm) pieces	2	2
Red medium pepper, seeds and ribs removed, cut into 1 inch (2.5 cm) pieces	1	1
Grated medium Cheddar cheese, for garnish		

(continued on next page)

Layer first 7 ingredients, in order given, in 5 to 7 quart (5 to 7 L) slow cooker.

Combine next 8 ingredients in medium bowl. Pour over tomatoes. Do not stir. Cover. Cook on Low for 8 to 10 hours or on High for 4 to 5 hours.

Add zucchini and red pepper. Stir well. Cover. Cook on High for 20 to 25 minutes until red pepper is tender-crisp. Makes about 11 cups (2.75 L) chili.

Garnish individual servings with cheese. Serves 8.

***1 serving:** 149 Calories; 1.6 g Total Fat (0.3 g Mono, 0.7 g Poly, 0.2 g Sat); 0 mg Cholesterol; 31 g Carbohydrate; 6 g Fibre; 6 g Protein; 470 mg Sodium*

Pictured on front cover.

Make Ahead: The night before, assemble first 15 ingredients, as directed, in slow cooker liner. Cover. Chill overnight. Cook as directed.

Paré Pointer

Don't hang funny pictures on the wall in case the plaster cracks up.

Veggie Lentil Stew

A rich, tomato-based stew packed with earthy lentils and vegetables. Perfect with whole-grain bread.

Dried green lentils, rinsed and drained	2 1/4 cups	550 mL
Medium carrots, quartered lengthwise, cut into 2 inch (5 cm) pieces	4	4
Medium leeks (white part only), halved lengthwise, cut into 1/2 inch (12 mm) slices	3	3
Chopped celery	1 cup	250 mL
Cubed red potato (with skin)	2 cups	500 mL
Garlic cloves, minced (or 1/2 tsp., 2 mL, powder), optional	2	2
Can of diced tomatoes (with juice)	28 oz.	796 mL
Prepared vegetable broth	3 cups	750 mL
Can of condensed cream of mushroom soup (or your favourite)	10 oz.	284 mL
Tomato juice	3/4 cup	175 mL
Dried basil	3/4 tsp.	4 mL
Dried thyme	1/2 tsp.	2 mL
Pepper	1/2 tsp.	2 mL

Measure lentils into 5 to 7 quart (5 to 7 L) slow cooker.

Layer next 5 ingredients, in order given, on top of lentils.

Combine remaining 7 ingredients in large bowl. Pour over vegetables. Do not stir. Cover. Cook on Low for 9 to 10 hours or on High for 4 1/2 to 5 hours. Serves 8.

1 serving: *353 Calories; 4.2 g Total Fat (0.8 g Mono, 1.9 g Poly, 1.1 g Sat); 0 mg Cholesterol; 61 g Carbohydrate; 11 g Fibre; 21 g Protein; 914 mg Sodium*

Make Ahead: The night before, assemble all 13 ingredients, as directed, in slow cooker liner. Cover. Chill overnight. Cook as directed.

Paré Pointer

The son said he'd be good for ten dollars.
The father at that age was good for nothing.

Tomato Bean Soup

A hearty, deep red tomato soup full of tender beans and vegetables. Top individual servings with a dollop of sour cream and serve with slices of crusty whole wheat bread.

Dried chickpeas (garbanzo beans), rinsed and drained	**1 cup**	**250 mL**
Dried red kidney beans, rinsed and drained	**1 cup**	**250 mL**
Boiling water		
Chopped onion	**1 cup**	**250 mL**
Chopped celery	**1 cup**	**250 mL**
Chopped carrot	**1 cup**	**250 mL**
Ground cumin	**1 tbsp.**	**15 mL**
Paprika	**1 tbsp.**	**15 mL**
Ground coriander	**1 tbsp.**	**15 mL**
Garlic cloves, minced (or 1/2 tsp., 2 mL, powder)	**2**	**2**
Prepared chicken (or vegetable) broth	**6 cups**	**1.5 L**
Can of diced tomatoes (with juice)	**28 oz.**	**796 mL**
Tomato paste (see Tip, page 13)	**2 tbsp.**	**30 mL**
Granulated sugar	**1 tsp.**	**5 mL**
Salt, sprinkle		
Box of frozen chopped spinach, thawed and squeezed dry	**10 oz.**	**284 mL**

Measure chickpeas and kidney beans into large bowl. Add boiling water until 2 inches (5 cm) above beans. Cover. Let stand for at least 1 hour until cool. Drain. Rinse beans. Drain well. Transfer to 5 to 7 quart (5 to 7 L) slow cooker.

Layer next 3 ingredients, in order given, on top of beans.

Sprinkle next 4 ingredients over carrot. Add broth. Do not stir. Cover. Cook on Low for 8 to 10 hours or on High for 4 to 5 hours.

Add next 4 ingredients. Stir well. Cover. Cook on High for about 30 minutes until heated through.

Add spinach. Stir well. Cover. Cook for 1 to 2 minutes until spinach is wilted. Makes about 12 1/2 cups (3.1 L).

1 cup (250 mL): *171 Calories; 2.4 g Total Fat (0.6 g Mono, 0.9 g Poly, 0.4 g Sat); 0 mg Cholesterol; 28 g Carbohydrate; 6 g Fibre; 11 g Protein; 535 mg Sodium*

Make Ahead: The night before, prepare beans as directed. Assemble with next 8 ingredients, as directed, in slow cooker liner. Cover. Chill overnight. Cook as directed.

White Bean Borscht

Creamy beet and bean soup with a dash of dill.
Sour cream and fresh parsley garnishes are a nice touch.

Dried navy beans, rinsed and drained	**1 cup**	**250 mL**
Boiling water		
Prepared chicken (or vegetable) broth	**8 cups**	**2 L**
Fresh medium beets, peeled, cut into 1/2 inch (12 mm) pieces	**3**	**3**
Finely chopped onion	**1 cup**	**250 mL**
Diced carrot	**2/3 cup**	**150 mL**
Finely chopped brown (or white) mushrooms	**1/2 cup**	**125 mL**
Garlic clove, minced (or 1/4 tsp., 1 mL, powder), optional	**1**	**1**
Bay leaf	**1**	**1**
Half-and-half cream	**1/2 cup**	**125 mL**
All-purpose flour	**2 tbsp.**	**30 mL**
Lemon juice	**1 tbsp.**	**15 mL**
Dill weed	**1 tsp.**	**5 mL**
Salt	**1 tsp.**	**5 mL**
Pepper	**1/2 tsp.**	**2 mL**

Sour cream (or half-and-half cream), for garnish
Chopped fresh parsley, for garnish

Measure beans into medium bowl. Add boiling water until 2 inches (5 cm) above beans. Cover. Let stand for at least 1 hour until cool. Drain. Rinse beans. Drain well. Transfer to 4 to 5 quart (4 to 5 L) slow cooker.

Add next 7 ingredients. Stir well. Cover. Cook on Low for 9 to 12 hours or on High for 4 1/2 to 6 hours. Remove and discard bay leaf.

Stir cream into flour in small bowl until smooth. Add to bean mixture. Stir well. Cover. Cook on High for about 15 minutes until boiling and slightly thickened.

Add next 4 ingredients. Stir well.

(continued on next page)

Garnish individual servings with sour cream and parsley. Makes about 9 3/4 cups (2.4 L).

1 cup (250 mL): 155 Calories; 2.9 g Total Fat (0.9 g Mono, 0.5 g Poly, 1.2 g Sat); 4 mg Cholesterol; 22 g Carbohydrate; 5 g Fibre; 10 g Protein; 964 mg Sodium

Make Ahead: The night before, prepare beans as directed. Assemble with next 7 ingredients, as directed, in slow cooker liner. Cover. Chill overnight. Cook as directed.

Chicken And Beans

A bit of bacon adds a satisfying smoky flavour to this filling dish.

Bacon slices, diced	**8**	**8**
All-purpose flour	**2 tbsp.**	**30 mL**
Boneless, skinless chicken thighs, halved	**1 lb.**	**454 g**
Can of diced tomatoes (with juice)	**28 oz.**	**796 mL**
Can of white kidney beans, rinsed and drained	**19 oz.**	**540 mL**
Chopped red pepper	**1 1/2 cups**	**375 mL**
Chopped onion	**1 cup**	**250 mL**
Salt	**1/4 tsp.**	**1 mL**
Pepper	**1/4 tsp.**	**1 mL**

Cook bacon in large frying pan on medium until almost crisp. Remove to paper towels to drain. Remove and discard drippings, reserving 1 tbsp. (15 mL) in pan.

Measure flour into large resealable freezer bag. Add 1/2 of chicken. Seal bag. Toss until coated. Repeat with remaining chicken. Heat reserved drippings in same large frying pan on medium. Add chicken in 2 batches. Cook for 8 to 10 minutes per batch, stirring occasionally, until browned. Transfer to 3 1/2 to 4 quart (3.5 to 4 L) slow cooker.

Combine bacon and remaining 6 ingredients in large bowl. Pour over chicken. Do not stir. Cover. Cook on Low for 8 to 10 hours or on High for 4 to 5 hours. Serves 4.

1 serving: 389 Calories; 13.4 g Total Fat (5 g Mono, 2.7 g Poly, 3.9 g Sat); 105 mg Cholesterol; 34 g Carbohydrate; 8 g Fibre; 34 g Protein; 834 mg Sodium

Pictured on page 125.

Make Ahead: The night before, prepare tomato mixture. Chill overnight in covered bowl. Assemble and cook as directed.

Sausage White Bean Soup

A kaleidoscope of colour and a team of textures produce a wonderful medley of flavour! Make it in the morning, enjoy it for supper.

Bacon slices, diced	6	6
Chopped onion	1 cup	250 mL
Garlic cloves, minced (or 1/2 tsp., 2 mL, powder)	2	2
Prepared chicken broth	5 cups	1.25 L
Can of white kidney beans, rinsed and drained	19 oz.	540 mL
Chopped yam (or sweet potato)	2 cups	500 mL
Sweet (or regular) chili sauce	2 tbsp.	30 mL
Pepper	1/2 tsp.	2 mL
Cooking oil	1 tsp.	5 mL
Chorizo sausages, casings removed, chopped	2	2
Fresh spinach, stems removed, lightly packed	3 cups	750 mL
Chopped fresh parsley (or 2 1/4 tsp., 11 mL, flakes)	3 tbsp.	50 mL
Lemon juice	1 tbsp.	15 mL

Cook bacon in medium frying pan on medium until crisp. Remove to paper towels to drain. Remove and discard drippings, reserving 1 tbsp. (15 mL) in pan.

Add onion. Cook for 5 to 10 minutes, stirring often, until softened.

Add garlic. Heat and stir for about 1 minute until fragrant. Transfer to 3 1/2 to 4 quart (3.5 to 4 L) slow cooker.

Add bacon and next 5 ingredients. Stir well. Cover. Cook on Low for 8 to 10 hours or on High for 4 to 5 hours.

Heat cooking oil in same medium frying pan on medium. Add sausage. Cook for 8 to 10 minutes, stirring occasionally, until no longer pink. Drain. Add to bean mixture. Stir.

(continued on next page)

Add spinach and parsley. Stir well. Cover. Cook on High for about 15 minutes until spinach is wilted.

Add lemon juice. Stir well. Makes about 9 cups (2.25 L).

1 cup (250 mL): *239 Calories; 11.3 g Total Fat (5.3 g Mono, 1.3 g Poly, 4.1 g Sat); 22 mg Cholesterol; 21 g Carbohydrate; 5 g Fibre; 13 g Protein; 924 mg Sodium*

Sweet And Spicy Beans

Sweet, smoky tomato sauce coats a tasty mix of beans and bacon. Serve with your favourite pasta salad and buns.

Bacon slices, cooked almost crisp and chopped	**8**	**8**
Cans of baked beans in tomato sauce (14 oz., 398 mL, each)	**2**	**2**
Can of chickpeas (garbanzo beans), rinsed and drained	**19 oz.**	**540 mL**
Can of red kidney beans, rinsed and drained	**19 oz.**	**540 mL**
Finely chopped onion	**1 cup**	**250 mL**
Ketchup	**1 1/2 cups**	**375 mL**
Water	**1/2 cup**	**125 mL**
Fancy (mild) molasses	**1/4 cup**	**60 mL**
White vinegar	**1/4 cup**	**60 mL**
Brown sugar, packed	**2 tbsp.**	**30 mL**
Worcestershire sauce	**1 1/2 tbsp.**	**25 mL**
Hot pepper sauce	**2 – 3 tsp.**	**10 – 15 mL**

Combine first 5 ingredients in 3 1/2 to 4 quart (3.5 to 4 L) slow cooker.

Add remaining 7 ingredients. Stir well. Cover. Cook on Low for 8 to 10 hours or on High for 4 to 5 hours. Serves 8.

1 serving: *327 Calories; 4.8 g Total Fat (1.8 g Mono, 1.1 g Poly, 1.4 g Sat); 5 mg Cholesterol; 64 g Carbohydrate; 13 g Fibre; 14 g Protein; 1284 mg Sodium*

Make Ahead: The night before, assemble all 12 ingredients, as directed, in slow cooker liner. Cover. Chill overnight. Cook as directed.

Full-Of-Beans Turkey Pot

A mild curry-flavoured dish that's definitely full of beans!

Cans of sliced peaches in light syrup (with juice), 14 oz. (398 mL) each	**2**	**2**
Can of red kidney beans, rinsed and drained	**19 oz.**	**540 mL**
Can of white kidney beans, rinsed and drained	**19 oz.**	**540 mL**
Can of black beans, rinsed and drained	**19 oz.**	**540 mL**
Can of baked beans in tomato sauce	**14 oz.**	**398 mL**
Chopped green pepper	**1 cup**	**250 mL**
Chopped onion	**1 cup**	**250 mL**
Sweet (or regular) chili sauce	**1/2 cup**	**125 mL**
Curry powder	**1 tsp.**	**5 mL**
Boneless, skinless turkey thighs, cut into 1 inch (2.5 cm) pieces	**1 1/2 lbs.**	**680 g**

Combine first 9 ingredients in 5 to 7 quart (5 to 7 L) slow cooker.

Add turkey. Stir well. Cover. Cook on Low for 8 to 10 hours or on High for 4 to 5 hours. Serves 8.

1 serving: *341 Calories; 3.8 g Total Fat (0.1 g Mono, 0.4 g Poly, 0.2 g Sat); 0 mg Cholesterol; 54 g Carbohydrate; 12 g Fibre; 27 g Protein; 690 mg Sodium*

Pictured on page 125.

Make Ahead: The night before, combine first 9 ingredients in slow cooker liner. Cover. Chill overnight. Add turkey. Cook as directed.

1. Full-Of-Beans Turkey Pot, above
2. Chicken And Beans, page 121
3. Beef And Lentils, page 132

Props Courtesy Of: Casa Bugatti
Island Pottery Inc.
Out of the Fire Studio
Totally Bamboo
Treasure Barrel

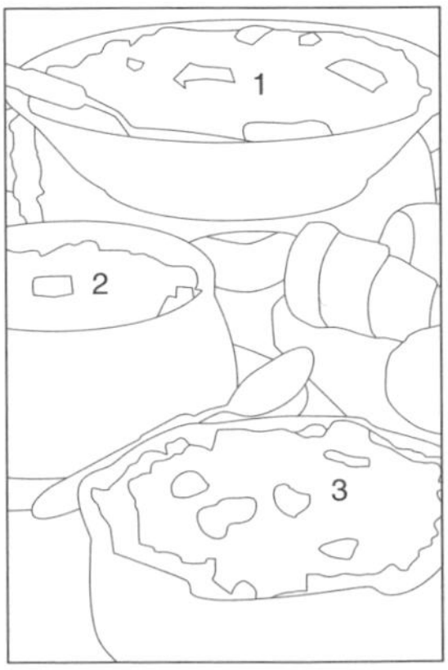

Red Lentil Soup

Smoky sausage adds flavour and substance to this filling soup. Serve with buns and salad for a delicious meal.

Water	**6 cups**	**1.5 L**
Dried red lentils, rinsed and drained	**2 cups**	**500 mL**
Diced garlic ham sausage	**1 1/2 cups**	**375 mL**
Chopped onion	**1 cup**	**250 mL**
Chopped carrot	**1 cup**	**250 mL**
Chopped celery	**1/2 cup**	**125 mL**
Basil pesto	**1 tbsp.**	**15 mL**
Bay leaves	**1 – 2**	**1 – 2**
Paprika	**1/2 tsp.**	**2 mL**
Pepper	**1/2 tsp.**	**2 mL**

Combine all 10 ingredients in 4 to 5 quart (4 to 5 L) slow cooker. Cover. Cook on Low for 8 to 10 hours or on High for 4 to 5 hours. Remove and discard bay leaves. Makes about 8 cups (2 L).

1 cup (250 mL): *248 Calories; 4.4 g Total Fat (0.4 g Mono, 0.5 g Poly, 0.1 g Sat); 0 mg Cholesterol; 34 g Carbohydrate; 6 g Fibre; 19 g Protein; 293 mg Sodium*

Make Ahead: The night before, combine all 10 ingredients in slow cooker liner. Cover. Chill overnight. Cook as directed.

1. Tomato Chickpea Pasta, page 130
2. Bacon Chicken Pasta, page 140
3. Meatballs In Sauce, page 22

Props Courtesy Of: Cherison Enterprises Inc.
Danesco Inc.
Out of the Fire Studio

Curried Split Pea Soup

This curried soup topped with croutons is sure to satisfy a dinnertime crowd.

Smoked pork hock (or meaty ham bone), about 1 3/4 lbs. (790 g)	**1**	**1**
Green split peas, rinsed and drained	**2 cups**	**500 mL**
Chopped onion	**1 cup**	**250 mL**
Chopped carrot	**1 cup**	**250 mL**
Chopped celery	**1 cup**	**250 mL**
Curry powder	**1 tbsp.**	**15 mL**
Dried thyme	**1 tsp.**	**5 mL**
Bay leaf	**1**	**1**
Pepper	**1/2 tsp.**	**2 mL**
Cans of condensed chicken broth (10 oz., 284 mL, each)	**2**	**2**
Water	**5 cups**	**1.25 L**
CURRIED CROUTONS		
White bread slices (with crusts), cubed	**6**	**6**
Grated Parmesan cheese	**2 tsp.**	**10 mL**
Curry powder	**1/2 tsp.**	**2 mL**
Hard margarine (or butter)	**1/4 cup**	**60 mL**

Put pork hock into 5 to 7 quart (5 to 7 L) slow cooker. Layer next 8 ingredients, in order given, over top.

Pour broth and water over top. Do not stir. Cover. Cook on Low for 8 to 10 hours or on High for 4 to 5 hours. Remove and discard bay leaf. Remove pork hock to cutting board. Let stand until cool enough to handle. Remove meat from bone. Discard bone. Cut meat into 1/2 inch (12 mm) pieces. Carefully process vegetable mixture with hand blender or in blender until smooth. Return meat to vegetable mixture. Stir well. Makes about 10 cups (2.5 L) soup.

Curried Croutons: Put bread cubes into large bowl. Add Parmesan cheese and curry powder. Toss well.

Melt margarine in large frying pan on medium. Add bread cube mixture. Heat and stir for about 10 minutes until bread cubes are toasted. Makes about 2 cups (500 mL) croutons. Divide and ladle soup into 8 individual bowls. Top each serving with 1/4 cup (60 mL) croutons. Serves 8.

(continued on next page)

1 serving: 441 Calories; 15.6 g Total Fat (8 g Mono, 1.9 g Poly, 4.4 g Sat); 39 mg Cholesterol; 47 g Carbohydrate; 5 g Fibre; 29 g Protein; 714 mg Sodium

Make Ahead: Croutons may be made ahead and stored in resealable container in freezer. Thaw before serving.

Hearty Winter Soup

Warm up with this chunky tomato soup thick with vegetables and bacon.

Bacon slices, cooked crisp and crumbled	**8**	**8**
Prepared chicken broth	**6 cups**	**1.5 L**
Chopped yellow turnip	**3 cups**	**750 mL**
Can of white kidney beans, rinsed and drained	**19 oz.**	**540 mL**
Chopped onion	**1 cup**	**250 mL**
Chopped carrot	**1 cup**	**250 mL**
Chopped celery	**1/2 cup**	**125 mL**
Tomato paste (see Tip, page 13)	**1/4 cup**	**60 mL**
Salt	**1/4 tsp.**	**1 mL**
Pepper	**1/4 tsp.**	**1 mL**
Frozen peas	**1 cup**	**250 mL**
Sprigs of fresh rosemary (see Note)	**2**	**2**
Chopped fresh parsley (or 1 1/2 tsp., 7 mL, flakes)	**2 tbsp.**	**30 mL**
Lemon juice	**1 tbsp.**	**15 mL**

Combine first 10 ingredients in 5 to 7 quart (5 to 7 L) slow cooker. Cover. Cook on Low for 9 to 10 hours or on High for 4 1/2 to 5 hours.

Add remaining 4 ingredients. Stir well. Cover. Cook on High for about 10 minutes until peas are heated through. Remove and discard rosemary sprigs. Makes about 11 cups (2.75 L).

1 cup (250 mL): 119 Calories; 3.4 g Total Fat (1.5 g Mono, 0.6 g Poly, 1.1 g Sat); 4 mg Cholesterol; 15 g Carbohydrate; 4 g Fibre; 8 g Protein; 690 mg Sodium

Pictured on page 143.

Note: Omit rosemary sprigs. Add 1/2 tsp. (2 mL) dried crushed rosemary to first 10 ingredients.

Make Ahead: The night before, combine first 10 ingredients in slow cooker liner. Cover. Chill overnight. Cook as directed.

Tomato Chickpea Pasta

Spicy chickpea and tomato sauce tossed with penne pasta.
A great way to introduce legumes!

Can of diced tomatoes (with juice)	**28 oz.**	**796 mL**
Can of chickpeas (garbanzo beans), rinsed and drained	**19 oz.**	**540 mL**
Dry white (or alcohol-free) wine	**1/2 cup**	**125 mL**
Olive (or cooking) oil	**2 tbsp.**	**30 mL**
Balsamic vinegar	**1 tbsp.**	**15 mL**
Garlic cloves, minced (or 1/2 tsp., 2 mL, powder)	**2**	**2**
Dried crushed chilies	**1/2 – 1 tsp.**	**2 – 5 mL**
Granulated sugar	**1/2 tsp.**	**2 mL**
Salt	**1/4 tsp.**	**1 mL**
Pepper	**1/4 tsp.**	**1 mL**
Chopped fresh parsley (or 2 1/4 tsp., 11 mL, flakes)	**3 tbsp.**	**50 mL**
Penne pasta (about 10 oz., 285 g)	**3 cups**	**750 mL**
Boiling water	**12 cups**	**3 L**
Salt	**1 1/2 tsp.**	**7 mL**
Grated Parmesan cheese	**1/3 cup**	**75 mL**

Combine first 10 ingredients in 3 1/2 to 4 quart (3.5 to 4 L) slow cooker. Cover. Cook on Low for 8 to 9 hours or on High for 4 to 4 1/2 hours.

Add parsley. Stir well.

Cook pasta in boiling water and second amount of salt in large uncovered pot or Dutch oven for 8 to 10 minutes, stirring occasionally, until tender but firm. Drain. Return pasta to pot. Add tomato mixture. Toss until coated. Remove to large serving bowl.

Sprinkle with Parmesan cheese. Serves 6.

1 serving: *354 Calories; 8.5 g Total Fat (4.3 g Mono, 1.3 g Poly, 2 g Sat); 5 mg Cholesterol; 54 g Carbohydrate; 4 g Fibre; 13 g Protein; 531 mg Sodium*

Pictured on page 126.

Make Ahead: The night before, combine first 10 ingredients in slow cooker liner. Cover. Chill overnight. Cook as directed.

Beans And Fennel

A wholesome, hearty mix of beans, fennel and spicy sausage deliciously dotted with dill. Serve with a crisp salad.

Fennel bulb (white part only), thinly sliced	1	1
Finely chopped carrot	1 cup	250 mL
Thinly sliced red onion	1 cup	250 mL
Cooking oil	1 tsp.	5 mL
Chorizo sausages, casings removed, cut into 1/2 inch (12 mm) slices	3	3
Can of diced tomatoes (with juice)	28 oz.	796 mL
Can of chickpeas (garbanzo beans), rinsed and drained	19 oz.	540 mL
Can of white kidney beans, rinsed and drained	19 oz.	540 mL
Can of romano beans, rinsed and drained	19 oz.	540 mL
Balsamic vinegar	1 tbsp.	15 mL
Granulated sugar	1 tsp.	5 mL
Salt	1/4 tsp.	1 mL
Pepper	1/2 tsp.	2 mL
Chopped fresh dill (or 1 1/2 tsp., 7 mL, dill weed)	2 tbsp.	30 mL

Layer fennel, carrot and onion in 4 to 5 quart (4 to 5 L) slow cooker.

Heat cooking oil in large frying pan on medium. Add sausage. Cook for 8 to 10 minutes, stirring occasionally, until browned. Drain. Set aside.

Combine next 8 ingredients in large bowl. Pour over vegetables. Do not stir. Scatter sausage over top. Cover. Cook on Low for 8 to 10 hours or on High for 4 to 5 hours.

Add dill. Stir well. Serves 8.

__1 serving:__ 315 Calories; 13.6 g Total Fat (6.1 g Mono, 1.7 g Poly, 4.8 g Sat); 28 mg Cholesterol; 33 g Carbohydrate; 6 g Fibre; 17 g Protein; 874 mg Sodium

Make Ahead: The night before, prepare vegetables and prepare tomato mixture. Chill overnight in separate covered bowls. Assemble and cook as directed.

Beef And Lentils

Tangy tomato and barbecue flavours add zip to ground beef and lentils. Simple to prepare. Serve on its own or over rice.

Can of diced tomatoes (with juice)	**28 oz.**	**796 mL**
Can of lentils, rinsed and drained	**19 oz.**	**540 mL**
Finely chopped onion	**1 1/2 cups**	**375 mL**
Finely chopped celery	**1/2 cup**	**125 mL**
Barbecue sauce	**3 tbsp.**	**50 mL**
Sweet (or regular) chili sauce	**2 1/2 tbsp.**	**37 mL**
Balsamic vinegar	**1 tbsp.**	**15 mL**
Bay leaf	**1**	**1**
Salt	**1/4 tsp.**	**1 mL**
Pepper	**1/8 tsp.**	**0.5 mL**
Cooking oil	**2 tsp.**	**10 mL**
Lean ground beef	**1 lb.**	**454 g**
All-purpose flour	**1 1/2 tbsp.**	**25 mL**
Prepared beef broth	**1/4 cup**	**60 mL**
Finely chopped fresh parsley (or 2 1/4 tsp., 11 mL, flakes), optional	**3 tbsp.**	**50 mL**

Combine first 10 ingredients in 3 1/2 to 4 quart (3.5 to 4 L) slow cooker.

Heat cooking oil in large frying pan on medium. Add ground beef. Scramble-fry for 5 to 10 minutes until no longer pink. Drain.

Sprinkle flour over beef. Heat and stir on medium for 1 minute. Slowly add broth, stirring constantly and scraping any brown bits from bottom of pan. Add to tomato mixture. Stir well. Cover. Cook on Low for 8 to 10 hours or on High for 4 to 5 hours. Remove and discard bay leaf.

Add parsley. Stir well. Serves 6.

***1 serving:** 298 Calories; 13.7 g Total Fat (6 g Mono, 1.2 g Poly, 4.8 g Sat); 42 mg Cholesterol; 24 g Carbohydrate; 5 g Fibre; 21 g Protein; 688 mg Sodium*

Pictured on page 125.

Make Ahead: The night before, combine first 10 ingredients, as directed, in slow cooker liner. Cover. Chill overnight. Scramble-fry ground beef until no longer pink. Drain. Chill overnight in covered bowl. Assemble and cook as directed.

Big Batch Bean Soup

You'll need a 7 quart (7 L) slow cooker for this soup, or recipe can be divided in half to fit a 3 1/2 to 4 quart (3.5 to 4 L) slow cooker. A great soup to freeze in individual containers to take to work or school.

Dried mixed beans (your choice)	**2 1/2 cups**	**625 mL**
Boiling water		
Prepared chicken (or vegetable) broth	**12 cups**	**3 L**
Bag of coleslaw mix	**16 oz.**	**500 mL**
Finely chopped onion	**1 cup**	**250 mL**
Chopped celery	**1 cup**	**250 mL**
Diced carrot	**1 cup**	**250 mL**
Dried marjoram	**1 tsp.**	**5 mL**
Dried thyme	**1 tsp.**	**5 mL**
Bay leaf	**1**	**1**
Pepper	**1/2 tsp.**	**2 mL**
Cans of stewed tomatoes (with juice), 14 oz. (398 mL) each, chopped	**2**	**2**
Chopped smoked ham sausage	**2 cups**	**500 mL**

Measure beans into large bowl. Add boiling water until 2 inches (5 cm) above beans. Cover. Let stand for at least 1 hour until cool. Drain. Rinse beans. Drain well. Transfer to 7 quart (7 L) slow cooker.

Add next 9 ingredients. Stir well. Cover. Cook on Low for 10 to 12 hours or on High for 5 to 6 hours. Remove and discard bay leaf.

Add tomatoes and sausage. Stir well. Cover. Cook on High for about 20 minutes until heated through. Makes about 22 cups (5.5 L).

1 cup (250 mL): *142 Calories; 3 g Total Fat (0.4 g Mono, 0.4 g Poly, 0.3 g Sat); 0 mg Cholesterol; 19 g Carbohydrate; 5 g Fibre; 11 g Protein; 697 mg Sodium*

Make Ahead: The night before, prepare beans as directed. Assemble with next 9 ingredients, as directed, in slow cooker liner. Cover. Chill overnight. Cook as directed.

Lamb And Bean Hot Pot

Rosemary adds just the right touch to this well-seasoned dish. The answer to dinner when there's company scheduled to arrive just after you do!

All-purpose flour	3 tbsp.	50 mL
Lamb loin chops (about 2 1/2 lbs., 1.1 kg)	12	12
Cooking oil	1 tbsp.	15 mL
Medium potatoes, peeled, cut into 1/4 inch (6 mm) slices	2	2
Sliced carrot	1 1/3 cups	325 mL
Thinly sliced onion	1 cup	250 mL
Salt	1/2 tsp.	2 mL
Pepper	1/2 tsp.	2 mL
Can of white kidney beans, rinsed and drained	19 oz.	540 mL
Prepared chicken broth	1 cup	250 mL
Dry sherry	1/2 cup	125 mL
Chopped fresh rosemary leaves (or 3/4 tsp., 4 mL, dried, crushed)	1 tbsp.	15 mL
Grated lemon zest	1 tsp.	5 mL
Granulated sugar	1 tsp.	5 mL
Worcestershire sauce	1 tsp.	5 mL
Chopped fresh mint leaves (or 3/4 tsp., 4 mL, dried), for garnish	1 tbsp.	15 mL

Measure flour into large resealable freezer bag. Add 1/2 of lamb chops. Seal bag. Toss until coated. Repeat with remaining lamb chops. Heat cooking oil in large frying pan on medium-high. Add lamb chops in 2 batches. Cook for about 3 minutes per batch, turning occasionally, until browned.

Layer potato, carrot and onion, in order given, in 4 to 5 quart (4 to 5 L) slow cooker. Sprinkle with salt and pepper. Arrange lamb chops, slightly overlapping, on top of onion.

Combine next 7 ingredients in medium bowl. Pour over lamb chops. Do not stir. Cover. Cook on Low for 8 to 10 hours or on High for 4 to 5 hours. Transfer lamb chops to large plate. Remove vegetable mixture with slotted spoon to large serving platter. Arrange lamb chops on top of vegetables.

(continued on next page)

Sprinkle with mint. Serves 6.

1 serving: *490 Calories; 26.3 g Total Fat (11.3 g Mono, 2.6 g Poly, 10.2 g Sat); 101 mg Cholesterol; 27 g Carbohydrate; 5 g Fibre; 32 g Protein; 552 mg Sodium*

Make Ahead: The night before, slice vegetables (except potatoes) and prepare kidney bean mixture. Chill overnight in separate covered bowls. Assemble and cook as directed.

Pea And Ham Soup

A light, satisfying split pea soup, that's sure to delight! You'll need a 5 to 7 quart (5 to 7 L) slow cooker for this large-quantity recipe. Freezes well.

Smoked pork hock (or meaty ham bone), about 1 3/4 lbs. (790 g)	**1**	**1**
Chopped onion	**2 cups**	**500 mL**
Chopped carrot	**2 cups**	**500 mL**
Chopped celery	**1 cup**	**250 mL**
Chopped parsnip	**1 cup**	**250 mL**
Yellow split peas, rinsed and drained	**2 1/4 cups**	**550 mL**
Bay leaves	**2**	**2**
Salt	**2 tsp.**	**10 mL**
Pepper	**1/2 tsp.**	**2 mL**
Water	**10 cups**	**2.5 L**

Put pork hock into 5 to 7 quart (5 to 7 L) slow cooker. Layer next 8 ingredients, in order given, over top.

Add water. Do not stir. Cover. Cook on Low for 9 to 10 hours or on High for 4 1/2 to 5 hours. Remove and discard bay leaves. Remove pork hock to cutting board. Let stand until cool enough to handle. Remove meat from bone. Discard bone. Coarsely chop meat. Return meat to vegetable mixture. Stir well. Cover. Cook on High for 10 to 15 minutes until heated through. Makes about 15 cups (3.74 L).

1 cup (250 mL): *186 Calories; 4.1 g Total Fat (1.7 g Mono, 0.5 g Poly, 1.4 g Sat); 19 mg Cholesterol; 25 g Carbohydrate; 4 g Fibre; 14 g Protein; 357 mg Sodium*

Make Ahead: The night before, prepare vegetables. Chill overnight in separate covered bowls. Assemble and cook as directed.

Short Ribs

They may be short in size, but they're long on taste!
Serve these saucy ribs with baked potatoes and all the fixings.

All-purpose flour	1 tbsp.	15 mL
Beef short ribs, bone-in, trimmed of fat	1 lb.	454 g
Chopped onion	1/2 cup	125 mL
Ketchup	1/4 cup	60 mL
Water	2 tbsp.	30 mL
White vinegar	2 tsp.	10 mL
Brown sugar, packed	2 tsp.	10 mL
Beef bouillon powder	1 tsp.	5 mL
Worcestershire sauce	1/2 tsp.	2 mL
Dry mustard	1/4 tsp.	1 mL
Liquid gravy browner	1/4 tsp.	1 mL
Liquid smoke	1/4 tsp.	1 mL
Salt	1/2 tsp.	2 mL
Pepper	1/8 tsp.	0.5 mL

Measure flour into large resealable freezer bag. Add ribs. Seal bag. Toss until coated. Transfer to 1 1/2 quart (1.5 L) slow cooker.

Scatter onion over top.

Combine remaining 11 ingredients in small bowl. Pour over onion. Do not stir. Cover. Cook on Low for 8 to 10 hours or on High for 4 to 5 hours. Serves 2.

***1 serving:** 255 Calories; 10 g Total Fat (4.3 g Mono, 0.5 g Poly, 4.2 g Sat); 45 mg Cholesterol; 21 g Carbohydrate; 1 g Fibre; 20 g Protein; 1380 mg Sodium*

Make Ahead: The night before, chop onion and prepare ketchup mixture. Chill overnight in separate covered bowls. Assemble and cook as directed.

Paré Pointer

We would all turn red like a stoplight
if we had to change in the middle of the street.

Stew For Two

Just me and you—it's stew for two.
Just you and me—not quite enough for three.

Baby potatoes, larger ones cut in half	10	10
Baby carrots, halved crosswise	8	8
Chopped onion	1/2 cup	125 mL
Small yellow turnip, cut into 1 inch (2.5 cm) pieces	1	1
Celery slices, 1/2 inch (12 mm) long	12	12
All-purpose flour	1 tbsp.	15 mL
Beef stew meat, cut into 3/4 inch (2 cm) pieces	1/2 lb.	225 g
Frozen peas	1/2 cup	125 mL
Can of tomato sauce	7 1/2 oz.	213 mL
Water	1/3 cup	75 mL
Granulated sugar	1/2 tsp.	2 mL
Salt	1/2 tsp.	2 mL
Pepper	1/8 tsp.	0.5 mL

Layer first 5 ingredients, in order given, in 1 1/2 quart (1.5 L) slow cooker.

Measure flour into large resealable freezer bag. Add beef. Seal bag. Toss until coated. Scatter beef over celery.

Scatter peas over beef.

Combine remaining 5 ingredients in small bowl. Pour over peas. Do not stir. Cover. Cook on Low for 8 to 10 hours or on High for 4 to 5 hours. Serves 2.

1 serving: *469 Calories; 10.5 g Total Fat (4.2 g Mono, 0.7 g Poly, 4.1 g Sat); 62 mg Cholesterol; 62 g Carbohydrate; 10 g Fibre; 34 g Protein; 1462 mg Sodium*

Make Ahead: The night before, cut up vegetables (except potatoes) and prepare tomato sauce mixture. Chill overnight in separate covered bowls. Assemble and cook as directed.

Steak Roll

A little bit fancier for a special occasion. Terrific served with roasted potatoes or rice and your favourite steamed vegetables.

Rouladen steak (1/4 inch, 6 mm, thick)	**8 oz.**	**225 g**
Salt, sprinkle		
Pepper, sprinkle		
Red pepper strips, each about 1/2 inch (12 mm) wide	**2**	**2**
Small carrot (about 4 inches, 10 cm), quartered lengthwise	**1**	**1**
Celery rib (about 4 inches, 10 cm), halved lengthwise	**1**	**1**
Onion slice (1/4 inch, 6 mm, thick), halved, layers separated	**1**	**1**
All-purpose flour	**2 tsp.**	**10 mL**
Hot water	**1/2 cup**	**125 mL**
Beef bouillon powder	**1 tsp.**	**5 mL**
Liquid gravy browner	**1/2 tsp.**	**2 mL**

Sprinkle steak with salt and pepper.

Layer next 4 ingredients crosswise in centre of steak. Roll up from short side to enclose vegetables. Tie roll with butcher's string or secure with metal skewers.

Dredge roll in flour in small shallow dish. Place in 1 1/2 quart (1.5 L) slow cooker.

Combine remaining 3 ingredients in 2 cup (500 mL) liquid measure. Pour over roll. Cover. Cook on Low for 8 to 10 hours or on High for 4 to 5 hours. Remove roll with slotted spoon to cutting board. Cut roll into 1 inch (2.5 cm) thick slices. Serves 2.

1 serving: *229 Calories; 10.3 g Total Fat (4.2 g Mono, 0.4 g Poly, 4.3 g Sat); 48 mg Cholesterol; 8 g Carbohydrate; 1 g Fibre; 25 g Protein; 429 mg Sodium*

Pictured on page 143.

Make Ahead: The night before, prepare vegetables. Chill overnight in separate covered bowls. Assemble and cook as directed.

Almost Meatloaf

Forgot to take meat out of the freezer? Nobody will mind (and they might not even notice) once they taste this smooth-textured loaf!

Creamed cottage cheese	**1 cup**	**250 mL**
Large eggs	**2**	**2**
Poultry seasoning	**3/4 tsp.**	**4 mL**
Dried basil	**1/2 tsp.**	**2 mL**
Salt	**1/2 tsp.**	**2 mL**
Pepper	**1/8 tsp.**	**0.5 mL**
Ground walnuts	**1 cup**	**250 mL**
Fine dry bread crumbs	**3/4 cup**	**175 mL**
Chopped onion	**1/2 cup**	**125 mL**
Grated part-skim mozzarella cheese	**1/2 cup**	**125 mL**
Ketchup	**2 tbsp.**	**30 mL**

Measure first 6 ingredients into medium bowl. Beat well.

Add next 4 ingredients. Stir well. Fold 17 inch (43 cm) length of foil lengthwise twice to make long strip 3 inches (7.5 cm) wide. Place in bottom and up side of 1 1/2 quart (1.5 L) slow cooker, allowing ends of foil strip to hang over side. Grease foil and inside of slow cooker with cooking spray. Press cottage cheese mixture evenly into slow cooker on top of foil strip.

Spread ketchup evenly over cottage cheese mixture. Cover. Cook on Low for 8 to 9 hours or on High for 4 to 4 1/2 hours. Run knife along inside edge of slow cooker, if necessary, to loosen. Holding ends of foil, carefully remove loaf to small serving platter. Discard foil. Cover loaf. Let stand for 10 minutes. Serves 4.

__1 serving:__ 364 Calories; 20.7 g Total Fat (5.5 g Mono, 8.8 g Poly, 5 g Sat); 125 mg Cholesterol; 25 g Carbohydrate; 3 g Fibre; 22 g Protein; 901 mg Sodium

Make Ahead: The night before, assemble all 11 ingredients, as directed, in slow cooker liner. Cover. Chill overnight. Cook as directed.

Bacon Chicken Pasta

Tender chicken and rotini pasta coated with a light, creamy sauce and a pungent pairing of feta cheese and smoky bacon. Serve with a crisp salad.

Bacon slices, diced	6	6
Chopped onion	1 cup	250 mL
Boneless, skinless chicken thighs, quartered	1 lb.	454 g
Prepared chicken broth	1 cup	250 mL
Salt	1/4 tsp.	1 mL
Pepper	1/2 tsp.	2 mL
Milk	1/2 cup	125 mL
Cornstarch	1 tbsp.	15 mL
Frozen peas	2/3 cup	150 mL
Chopped fresh parsley (or 1 1/2 tsp., 7 mL, flakes)	2 tbsp.	30 mL
Rotini (or other spiral) pasta (about 8 oz., 225 g)	3 cups	750 mL
Boiling water	8 cups	2 L
Salt	1 tsp.	5 mL
Crumbled feta cheese	1 cup	250 mL

Cook bacon in large frying pan on medium until almost crisp. Drain, reserving bacon and about 1 tsp. (5 mL) drippings in pan.

Add onion. Cook for 5 to 10 minutes, stirring often, until onion is softened. Transfer to 1 1/2 quart (1.5 L) slow cooker.

Add next 4 ingredients. Stir well. Cover. Cook on Low for 8 to 10 hours or on High for 4 to 5 hours.

Stir milk into cornstarch in small bowl until smooth. Add to chicken mixture. Stir.

(continued on next page)

Add peas and parsley. Stir well. Cover. Cook on High for 15 to 20 minutes until sauce is thickened.

Cook pasta in boiling water and second amount of salt in large uncovered pot or Dutch oven for 10 to 15 minutes, stirring occasionally, until tender but firm. Drain. Return pasta to pot.

Add chicken mixture and feta cheese. Toss gently until coated. Serves 4.

1 serving: *557 Calories; 18.8 g Total Fat (5.9 g Mono, 2.8 g Poly, 8.1 g Sat); 130 mg Cholesterol; 54 g Carbohydrate; 4 g Fibre; 40 g Protein; 882 mg Sodium*

Pictured on page 126.

Paré Pointer

A carpenter's favourite nail to watch for is a thumbnail.

Beef Barley Soup For Two

A fragrant, filling soup that's just enough for two.
Serve with buns and a crisp green salad.

Beef stew meat, cut into 1/2 inch (12 mm) pieces	**1/4 lb.**	**113 g**
Diced peeled potato	**1/4 cup**	**60 mL**
Diced carrot	**1/4 cup**	**60 mL**
Chopped onion	**1/4 cup**	**60 mL**
Chopped celery	**2 tbsp.**	**30 mL**
Pearl barley	**1 tbsp.**	**15 mL**
Water	**1 cup**	**250 mL**
Prepared beef broth	**2/3 cup**	**150 mL**
Tomato juice	**2/3 cup**	**150 mL**
Dried basil	**1/4 tsp.**	**1 mL**
Granulated sugar	**1/4 tsp.**	**1 mL**
Salt	**1/4 tsp.**	**1 mL**

Combine first 6 ingredients in 1 1/2 quart (1.5 L) slow cooker.

Measure remaining 6 ingredients into medium bowl. Stir. Add to beef mixture. Stir well. Cover. Cook on Low for 8 to 10 hours or on High for 4 to 5 hours. Makes about 3 cups (750 mL).

1 cup (250 mL): *120 Calories; 3.5 g Total Fat (1.5 g Mono, 0.2 g Poly, 1.4 g Sat); 21 mg Cholesterol; 12 g Carbohydrate; 2 g Fibre; 10 g Protein; 621 mg Sodium*

Make Ahead: The night before, prepare vegetables (except potato) and prepare broth mixture. Chill overnight in separate covered bowls. Assemble and cook as directed.

1. Steak Roll, page 138
2. Hearty Winter Soup, page 129

Props Courtesy Of: Casa Bugatti
Cherison Enterprises Inc.

Yam And Chops

Simple preparation and fine flavour. Just add a salad, and dinner's ready!

Yams (or sweet potatoes), peeled, cubed	**3/4 lb.**	**340 g**
Soy sauce	**1 tsp.**	**5 mL**
Lemon pepper	**1/2 tsp.**	**2 mL**
Garlic powder, just a pinch		
Boneless pork loin chops (about 1/2 lb., 225 g), trimmed of fat	**2**	**2**
Frozen kernel corn (or peas)	**2/3 cup**	**150 mL**

Put yam into 1 1/2 quart (1.5 L) slow cooker.

Combine soy sauce, lemon pepper and garlic powder in small cup.

Blot pork chops with paper towels. Brush soy sauce mixture on both sides of each chop. Place chops on top of yam.

Scatter corn over top. Cover. Cook on Low for 8 to 9 hours or on High for 4 to 4 1/2 hours. Serves 2.

1 serving: *385 Calories; 6.7 g Total Fat (2.8 g Mono, 1 g Poly, 2.2 g Sat); 62 mg Cholesterol; 53 g Carbohydrate; 7 g Fibre; 29 g Protein; 536 mg Sodium*

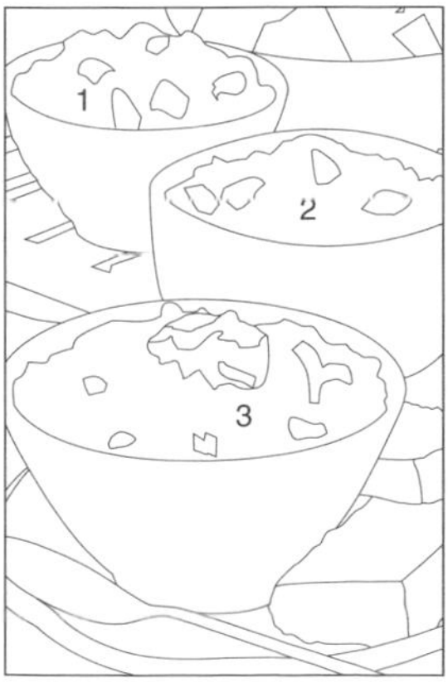

1. Mild Turkey Chili, page 56
2. Chili Chicken, page 146
3. Chili Black Beans, page 115

Props Courtesy Of: Cherison Enterprises Inc.

Chili Chicken

Spicy and sweet. Everyone will love this saucy stew.

All-purpose flour	**2 tbsp.**	**30 mL**
Boneless, skinless chicken thighs, halved	**1 lb.**	**454 g**
Cooking oil	**1 tbsp.**	**15 mL**
Can of diced tomatoes (with juice)	**14 oz.**	**398 mL**
Chopped red pepper	**1 cup**	**250 mL**
Frozen kernel corn	**1 cup**	**250 mL**
Chopped onion	**2/3 cup**	**150 mL**
Chipotle chili pepper, chopped (see Tip, page 95)	**1**	**1**
Salt	**1/4 tsp.**	**1 mL**
Sour cream	**3 tbsp.**	**50 mL**
Chopped fresh cilantro or parsley (or 1 1/2 tsp., 7 mL, dried)	**2 tbsp.**	**30 mL**

Measure flour into large resealable freezer bag. Add chicken. Seal bag. Toss until coated. Heat cooking oil in large frying pan on medium. Add chicken. Cook for 8 to 10 minutes, turning occasionally, until browned. Transfer to 1 1/2 quart (1.5 L) slow cooker.

Add next 6 ingredients. Stir well. Cover. Cook on Low for 8 to 10 hours or on High for 4 to 5 hours.

Add sour cream and cilantro. Stir well. Cover. Cook on High for about 5 minutes until heated through. Serves 4.

1 serving: *294 Calories; 11.9 g Total Fat (4.5 g Mono, 3 g Poly, 2.9 g Sat); 99 mg Cholesterol; 23 g Carbohydrate; 3 g Fibre; 26 g Protein; 322 mg Sodium*

Pictured on page 144.

Make Ahead: The night before, prepare tomato mixture. Chill overnight in covered bowl. Assemble and cook as directed.

Paré Pointer

No wonder monastery food is so greasy—the cooking is done by friars.

Beef Stroganoff

Serve this creamy beef dish over broad egg noodles for a traditional presentation. Good with rice, too.

All-purpose flour	1 tbsp.	15 mL
Paprika	1/4 tsp.	1 mL
Salt	1/4 tsp.	1 mL
Pepper	1/16 tsp.	0.5 mL
Beef round steak, cut into 1/4 inch (6 mm) strips	1/2 lb.	225 g
Chopped onion	1/2 cup	125 mL
Sliced fresh white mushrooms	1/2 cup	125 mL
Sour cream	1/2 cup	125 mL
All-purpose flour	1 tbsp.	15 mL
Water	1/2 cup	125 mL
Beef bouillon powder	1 tsp.	5 mL
Parsley flakes	1/2 tsp.	2 mL

Measure first 4 ingredients into large resealable freezer bag. Add beef. Seal bag. Toss until coated. Transfer beef to 1 1/2 quart (1.5 L) slow cooker. Sprinkle with any remaining flour mixture.

Add onion and mushrooms.

Stir sour cream into second amount of flour in small bowl until smooth. Add water, bouillon powder and parsley. Stir well. Pour over vegetables. Stir. Cover. Cook on Low for 8 to 9 hours or on High for 4 to 4 1/2 hours. Serves 2.

***1 serving:** 451 Calories; 15.4 g Total Fat (5.1 g Mono, 1.1 g Poly, 7.6 g Sat); 112 mg Cholesterol; 42 g Carbohydrate; 2 g Fibre; 35 g Protein; 692 mg Sodium*

Make Ahead: The night before, cut up vegetables and prepare sour cream mixture. Chill overnight in separate covered bowls. Assemble and cook as directed.

Borscht

Vegetables, beef and beets in an old family favourite.
Serve with a swirl of sour cream.

Lean ground beef	**1/4 lb.**	**113 g**
Shredded green (or red) cabbage, lightly packed	**1/3 cup**	**75 mL**
Chopped onion	**1/4 cup**	**60 mL**
Grated carrot	**2 tbsp.**	**30 mL**
Grated yellow turnip	**2 tbsp.**	**30 mL**
Fresh large beet, peeled, cut julienne	**1**	**1**
Water	**2 cups**	**500 mL**
Ketchup	**2 tbsp.**	**30 mL**
White vinegar	**1 tsp.**	**5 mL**
Granulated sugar	**1/2 tsp.**	**2 mL**
Parsley flakes	**1/2 tsp.**	**2 mL**
Dill weed	**1/8 tsp.**	**0.5 mL**
Bay leaf	**1/2**	**1/2**
Salt	**1/2 tsp.**	**2 mL**
Pepper	**1/8 tsp.**	**0.5 mL**

Scramble-fry ground beef in small frying pan on medium until no longer pink. Drain well.

Combine next 4 ingredients in large bowl. Add ground beef. Mix well.

Add beets. Mix gently. Transfer to 1 1/2 quart (1.5 L) slow cooker.

Measure remaining 9 ingredients into small bowl. Stir well. Add to beef mixture. Stir well. Cover. Cook on Low for 8 to 10 hours or on High for 4 to 5 hours. Remove and discard bay leaf half. Makes about 3 cups (750 mL).

1 cup (250 mL): *120 Calories; 5.8 g Total Fat (2.5 g Mono, 0.3 g Poly, 2.3 g Sat); 21 mg Cholesterol; 9 g Carbohydrate; 1 g Fibre; 8 g Protein; 574 mg Sodium*

Make Ahead: The night before, prepare vegetables and prepare ketchup mixture. Chill overnight in separate covered bowls. Assemble and cook as directed.

Baked Beans

You don't need to make a large amount to enjoy the rich flavour of baked beans. Serve with biscuits.

Dried navy beans, rinsed and drained	**1/2 cup**	**125 mL**
Boiling water		
Water	**1 2/3 cups**	**400 mL**
Chopped onion	**1/2 cup**	**125 mL**
Fancy (mild) molasses	**2 tbsp.**	**30 mL**
Brown sugar, packed	**2 tbsp.**	**30 mL**
Ketchup	**2 tbsp.**	**30 mL**
Dry mustard	**1/2 tsp.**	**2 mL**
Onion powder	**1/4 tsp.**	**1 mL**
Liquid smoke	**1/4 tsp.**	**1 mL**
White vinegar	**1/2 tsp.**	**2 mL**
Salt	**1/4 tsp.**	**1 mL**
Pepper, just a pinch		

Measure beans into medium bowl. Add boiling water until 2 inches (5 cm) above beans. Cover. Let stand for at least 1 hour until cool. Drain. Rinse beans. Drain well. Transfer to 1 1/2 quart (1.5 L) slow cooker.

Combine remaining 11 ingredients in medium bowl. Add to beans. Stir well. Cover. Cook on Low for 10 to 12 hours or on High for 5 to 6 hours. Serves 2.

1 serving: *329 Calories; 1.1 g Total Fat (0.3 g Mono, 0.4 g Poly, 0.2 g Sat); 0 mg Cholesterol; 70 g Carbohydrate; 10 g Fibre; 13 g Protein; 499 mg Sodium*

Make Ahead: The night before, prepare beans as directed. Assemble with next 11 ingredients, as directed, in slow cooker liner. Cover. Chill overnight. Cook as directed.

Paré Pointer

The only food Moby Dick ever wanted for his lunch was fish and ships.

Measurement Tables

Throughout this book measurements are given in Conventional and Metric measure. To compensate for differences between the two measurements due to rounding, a full metric measure is not always used. The cup used is the standard 8 fluid ounce. Temperature is given in degrees Fahrenheit and Celsius. Baking pan measurements are in inches and centimetres as well as quarts and litres. An exact metric conversion is given below as well as the working equivalent (Metric Standard Measure).

Oven Temperatures

Fahrenheit (°F)	Celsius (°C)
175°	80°
200°	95°
225°	110°
250°	120°
275°	140°
300°	150°
325°	160°
350°	175°
375°	190°
400°	205°
425°	220°
450°	230°
475°	240°
500°	260°

Pans

Conventional Inches	Metric Centimetres
8x8 inch	20x20 cm
9x9 inch	22x22 cm
9x13 inch	22x33 cm
10x15 inch	25x38 cm
11x17 inch	28x43 cm
8x2 inch round	20x5 cm
9x2 inch round	22x5 cm
10x4 1/2 inch tube	25x11 cm
8x4x3 inch loaf	20x10x7.5 cm
9x5x3 inch loaf	22x12.5x7.5 cm

Spoons

Conventional Measure	Metric Exact Conversion Millilitre (mL)	Metric Standard Measure Millilitre (mL)
1/8 teaspoon (tsp.)	0.6 mL	0.5 mL
1/4 teaspoon (tsp.)	1.2 mL	1 mL
1/2 teaspoon (tsp.)	2.4 mL	2 mL
1 teaspoon (tsp.)	4.7 mL	5 mL
2 teaspoons (tsp.)	9.4 mL	10 mL
1 tablespoon (tbsp.)	14.2 mL	15 mL

Cups

Conventional Measure	Metric Exact Conversion Millilitre (mL)	Metric Standard Measure Millilitre (mL)
1/4 cup (4 tbsp.)	56.8 mL	60 mL
1/3 cup (5 1/3 tbsp.)	75.6 mL	75 mL
1/2 cup (8 tbsp.)	113.7 mL	125 mL
2/3 cup (10 2/3 tbsp.)	151.2 mL	150 mL
3/4 cup (12 tbsp.)	170.5 mL	175 mL
1 cup (16 tbsp.)	227.3 mL	250 mL
4 1/2 cups	1022.9 mL	1000 mL (1 L)

Dry Measurements

Conventional Measure Ounces (oz.)	Metric Exact Conversion Grams (g)	Metric Standard Measure Grams (g)
1 oz.	28.3 g	28 g
2 oz.	56.7 g	57 g
3 oz.	85.0 g	85 g
4 oz.	113.4 g	125 g
5 oz.	141.7 g	140 g
6 oz.	170.1 g	170 g
7 oz.	198.4 g	200 g
8 oz.	226.8 g	250 g
16 oz.	453.6 g	500 g
32 oz.	907.2 g	1000 g (1 kg)

Casseroles

CANADA & BRITAIN		UNITED STATES	
Standard Size Casserole	Exact Metric Measure	Standard Size Casserole	Exact Metric Measure
1 qt. (5 cups)	1.13 L	1 qt. (4 cups)	900 mL
1 1/2 qts. (7 1/2 cups)	1.69 L	1 1/2 qts. (6 cups)	1.35 L
2 qts. (10 cups)	2.25 L	2 qts. (8 cups)	1.8 L
2 1/2 qts. (12 1/2 cups)	2.81 L	2 1/2 qts. (10 cups)	2.25 L
3 qts. (15 cups)	3.38 L	3 qts. (12 cups)	2.7 L
4 qts. (20 cups)	4.5 L	4 qts. (16 cups)	3.6 L
5 qts. (25 cups)	5.63 L	5 qts. (20 cups)	4.5 L

Recipe Index

D

E

F

G

H

J

L

M

O

P

R

T

V

W

Y

Z

Company's Coming cookbooks are available at retail locations throughout Canada!

EXCLUSIVE mail order offer on next page

Buy any 2 cookbooks—choose a 3rd FREE of equal or less value than the lowest price paid.

Original Series — CA$15.99 Canada — US$12.99 USA & International

CODE	
SQ	150 Delicious Squares
CA	Casseroles
MU	Muffins & More
SA	Salads
AP	Appetizers
SS	Soups & Sandwiches
CO	Cookies
PA	Pasta
BA	Barbecues
PR	Preserves
CH	Chicken, Etc.
KC	Kids Cooking
CT	Cooking For Two
SC	Slow Cooker Recipes

CODE	
ODM	One-Dish Meals
ST	Starters
SF	Stir-Fry
MAM	Make-Ahead Meals
PB	The Potato Book
CCLFC	Low-Fat Cooking
CCLFP	Low-Fat Pasta
CFK	Cook For Kids
SCH	Stews, Chilies & Chowders
FD	Fondues
CCBE	The Beef Book
CB	The Cheese Book
RC	The Rookie Cook
RHR	Rush-Hour Recipes

CODE	
SW	Sweet Cravings
YRG	Year Round Grilling
GG	Garden Greens
CHC	Chinese Cooking
PK	The Pork Book
RL	Recipes For Leftovers
EB	The Egg Book
SDPP	School Days Party Pack
HS	Herbs & Spices
BEV	The Beverage Book
SCD	Slow Cooker Dinners
WM	30-Minute Weekday Meals NEW *May 1/05*

Lifestyle Series

CODE	CA$17.99 Canada US$15.99 USA & International
DC	Diabetic Cooking

CODE	CA$19.99 Canada US$15.99 USA & International
HC	Heart-Friendly Cooking
DDI	Diabetic Dinners
LCR	Low-Carb Recipes NEW *March 1/05*

Special Occasion Series

CODE	CA$20.99 Canada US$19.99 USA & International
GFK	Gifts from the Kitchen

CODE	CA$22.99 Canada US$19.99 USA & International
WC	Weekend Cooking

CODE	CA$24.99 Canada US$19.99 USA & International
BSS	Baking—Simple to Sensational

Most Loved Recipe Collection

CODE	CA$23.99 Canada US$19.99 USA & International
MLA	Most Loved Appetizers
MLMC	Most Loved Main Courses
MLT	Most Loved Treats
MLBQ	Most Loved Barbecuing NEW *April 1/05*

Company's Coming® COOKBOOKS

Company's Coming Publishing Limited
2311 – 96 Street
Edmonton, Alberta, Canada T6N 1G3
Tel: 780-450-6223 Fax: 780-450-1857
www.companyscoming.com

EXCLUSIVE Mail Order Offer

See previous page for list of cookbooks

Buy 2 Get 1 FREE!
Buy any 2 cookbooks—choose a **3rd FREE** of equal or less value than the lowest price paid.

Quantity	Code	Title	Price Each	Price Total
			$	$
		DON'T FORGET		
		to indicate your FREE BOOK(S).		
		(see exclusive mail order		
		offer above) please print		

TOTAL BOOKS (including FREE)

TOTAL BOOKS PURCHASED: $

	International		Canada & USA	
Plus Shipping & Handling (per destination)	$ 6.99	(one book)	$ 3.99	(one book)
Additional Books (including FREE books)	$	($4.99 each)	$	($1.99 each)
Sub-Total	$		$	
Canadian residents add G.S.T.(7%)			$	
TOTAL AMOUNT ENCLOSED	$		$	

The Fine Print

- Orders outside Canada must be **PAID IN US FUNDS** by cheque or money order drawn on Canadian or US bank or by credit card.
- Make cheque or money order payable to: **Company's Coming Publishing Limited.**
- Prices are expressed in Canadian dollars for Canada, US dollars for USA & International and are subject to change without prior notice.
- Orders are shipped surface mail. For courier rates, visit our web-site: **www.companyscoming.com** or contact us: **Tel: 780-450-6223 Fax: 780-450-1857.**
- Sorry, no C.O.D.'s.

Gift Giving

- Let us help you with your gift giving!
- We will send cookbooks directly to the recipients of your choice if you give us their names and addresses.
- Please specify the titles you wish to send to each person.
- If you would like to include your personal note or card, we will be pleased to enclose it with your gift order.
- Company's Coming Cookbooks make excellent gifts: birthdays, bridal showers, Mother's Day, Father's Day, graduation or any occasion ...collect them all!

❒ MasterCard ❒ VISA

Expiry date

Account #

Name of cardholder

Cardholder's signature

Shipping Address

Send the cookbooks listed above to:

Name:

Street:

City: Prov./State:

Country: Postal Code/Zip:

Tel: ( )

Email address:

❒ YES! Please send a catalogue